"Nothing Happens Until The Meeting Is Set"

Connecting People, Business, & Products

With Tips On Effective And Proven Methods For Acquiring Sales Meetings

John McKee

Published by Richter Publishing LLC www.richterpublishing.com

Book Cover Design: Ruby Graphic Design

Editors: Mandi Weems & Kenny Darling

ISBN: 0692737677

ISBN-13: 9780692737675

DISCLAIMER

This book is designed to provide information on business meetings only. This information is provided and sold with the knowledge that the publisher and author do not offer any legal or medical advice. In the case of a need for any such expertise consult with the appropriate professional. This book does not contain all information available on the subject. This book has not been created to be specific to any individual people or organization's situation or needs. Reasonable efforts have been made to make this book as accurate as possible. However, there may be typographical and or content errors. Therefore, this book should serve only as a general guide . This book contains information that might be dated or erroneous and is intended only to educate and entertain. The author and publisher shall have no liability or responsibility to any person or entity regarding any loss or damage incurred, or alleged to have incurred, directly or indirectly, by the information contained in this book or as a result of anyone acting or failing to act upon the information in this book. You hereby agree never to sue and to hold the author and publisher harmless from any and all claims arising out of the information contained in this book. You hereby agree to be bound by this disclaimer, covenant not to sue and release. You may return this book within the guarantee time period for a full refund. In the interest of full disclosure, this book contains affiliate links that might pay the author or publisher a commission upon any purchase from the company. While the author and publisher take no responsibility for any virus or technical issues that could be caused by such links, the business practices of these companies and or the performance of any product or service, the author or publisher has used the product or service and makes a recommendation in good faith based on that experience. All characters appearing in this work are fictitious. Any resemblance to real persons, living or dead, is purely coincidental.

TESTIMONIALS

"John McKee gets it. A masterful story, part life and part career. McKee shares his 26 year business journey as he connects thousands of people, businesses and products though meetings. As a result and with mentorship and reading books he finds his niche as a key person of influence in business development. He shares his 5 Simple Steps and Proven Techniques to Arranging Meetings."

- Kevin Harrington, Shark from ABC's "Shark Tank"
http://kevinharrington.tv/

"Nothing Happens Until the Meeting is Set is a fascinating, lesson-filled read for any success-bound business person. It's a free flowing look into the mind of a true entrepreneur who doesn't mind putting himself out there - the good, the bad, and most of all, the useful - for you, the serious reader!"

- Steve Grant, Director of Dale Carnegie Training of Central Illinois www.centralil.dalecarnegie.com

"John's new book is an interesting and educational read about his life and journey in growing businesses. A great book for any aspiring business entrepreneur or startup. Filled with valuable lessons learned and useful sales tips."

-Jeff Hoffman Co-Founder of Priceline.com

DEDICATION

I dedicate this book to my daughter, Lauren McKee. I want to encourage her on the idea that you can do anything you want to do if you put your mind to it. Please do not let anyone or anything stand in your way or tell you can't, because anything is possible! I love you.

I'm also dedicating this book to my stepsons, Nathaniel and Alekzander Nixon. I hope they continue doing great things with their lives.

Also, I dedicate this book to my sisters, Janet and Karen, and their families, my friend Betty, and the team I've been working with the last seven years at Prairie Technology Alliance. I thank them for supporting me along the way.

I also want to include all my friends who have put up with my social media hype showcasing myself and advertising me, me, and me. Thank all of you for not deleting me. Additional acknowledgements are listed in the back and throughout the book.

I must also give credit and thanks to all the people who have inspired me with quotes, books, speeches, etc., and who had the ability to indirectly give me mentor guidance, most of which has been through their publications, social media, and some face to face meetings.

Guidance and inspiration in this book mainly comes from the member owners at Prairie Tech Alliance.

Quotes, articles, and videos by Daymond John of ABC's Shark Tank have also helped me tremendously along the way.

Quotes, articles, videos, books, KPI book and direct guidance from Kevin Harrington of ABC's Shark Tank, Patrick Bet-David, Gary Vanerchukand Grant Cardone have all been an inspiration in my career and personal life.

CONTENTS

ACKNOWLEDGMENTS

I believe in acknowledging people, and I tried to mention as many as I could in the beginning and throughout the book, but it's important to me to make sure they know and that I name them and thank all of them for their support, inspiration, and mentorship. All of those whose quotes I mentioned, which have inspired and helped get me through this, include (in no particular order):

To my late parents, Ruey McKee and Gordon McKee (for making me possible), my daughter Lauren McKee, stepsons Nathaniel and Alek Nixon, my sisters Janet and Karen McKee and their families for all their support; my best friend Betty Kelly and to business partners Troy McDaniel and Kevin Krosse, and to Brian Ford, Brad Juergens, Fred Dirkse, and Tom Simpson for making it possible for me to do what I do. And a quick thank you to Ruby Thompson for graphics.

To all of my friends, and the ones who I meet with on a regular basis over dinner and lunch, like Mike Haldeman and Paul Martin, when we discuss business, startups and life; and all my friends and connections on Facebook and LinkedIn for putting up with my self-promoting posts and for not deleting me, hopefully understanding it's all for business decisions and marketing purposes. I also want to thank Carolyn Gunn for guidance in my life.

To all my indirect mentors: Kevin Harrington, Patrick Bet David, Grant Cardone, Daymond John, the late Steve Jobs, Dale Tripp, Joe Bansazek, Tony Wolgemuth, and so many others who, unfortunately, I cannot remember all their names but are in my mind and heart, for making an impression or impact on me. Thanks to all my clients and business relationships for their business, our partnerships, and to everyone who purchased my book.

To all my past and current employers for their interest in me and for providing me with significant sales training, which I credit to helping form me into who I am.

To all of these people and businesses who have had an effect on me, in one way or another, and for mentioning them and their inspiring quotes: Will Smith, Connor McGregor, Doris Symonds, Thomas Edison, Tabatha Coffey, CEO of Tesla, Dave Alwan, Caleb Maddix, Dale Carnegie, K. Anders Ericsson, and Percy Whiting.

Score Mentors, Shark Tank, BTC.com, 1 Million Cups, Https://asseenontv.pro/, Empire Beauty school, Five Senses Salon, LinkedIn, Microsoft, KushAndWiZoom, Facebook, and Twitter

Finally, to all the local fast food restaurants for making it easy to get food when I am writing. I also do not want to forget all the Starbucks in my area, the Thirty-Thirty Coffee shop, and the local East Peoria Library for the use of their facilities while I write.

FOREWORD

Over the last 3 years, I have been interested in writing a book. Why does someone decide to do it? Are they anything like me? I didn't see the answer for myself until last year, and since, I have been encouraging others to do the same.

Encouraging others was my way of living through someone else to see if they could do it. I then wondered if I would have the courage to do this myself. Everyone always tells me they have thought about it but they do not have the time. There is a great quote to think about, however, in this regard: "One day, you will wake up and there won't be any more time to do the things you've always wanted. Do it now." I do not know who should receive credit for this quote, but I like it.

I have told several friends, and now I am telling many others, "Your life story is amazing. There are a lot of people that would be inspired by what you have done in your life." I often wondered if that would likewise be true of me. Would others be interested in what I have to say, what I have learned, and what I am good at? Will it help anyone?

At the early age of seven, I wrote several books at school and I still have one of them. I wrote a short, 21-page story about

Snoopy, the little bird called Woodstock, and the Red Baron from the Charlie Brown Series. I created my own story about a dog, his flying house, and going into battle with enemies with real airplanes and guns, and it included multiple pages detailing their daily lives.

I have no idea why I decided to write about those characters, but it was a school project. It was fun and I'll give the story to my daughter someday. Now 45 years later, I have written another book. I honestly do not have anything from my past that far back except for that Snoopy book.

I think it's very ironic looking back now, and I took it as a sign to write another book on this other side of my life. I have met people who have published books and interviewed several of them. I attended a product inventor's think tank, where I met an inspiring mentor and author Kevin Harrington. He encouraged a group of entrepreneurs to publish a book. Kevin Harrington is the Original Shark from Shark Tank & co-authored a book with Daniel Priestly "Key Person of Influence". I highly recommend the book. I met Mr. Harrington in person on December 9, 2015 in Coral Springs FL, and recently again in Des Moines, IA, on April 23, 2016. He laid out five points he contributes to his success and encouraged us all to do the same. "Get published," he says. Since I was already thinking about it upon hearing his advice and reading his book, a light bulb went off, and it convinced me that I was a good candidate to move forward. This encouraged me to publish this book on what I have learned.

Timing is everything. If you are looking for a sign to tell you to write a book, reading my book may be that sign. I can only hope that my lack of experience in writing doesn't show too much and that with each sentence or paragraph you will be able to relate, find interest, or somehow be inspired. "If this guy can do it, so can I," you might say. Because, like a lot of books I have read, some authors give a brief history on their background, I plan on doing the same.

Further Inspiration

If you are planning on writing a book, I suggest getting started when you have a large chunk of alone time, because no one will be able to interrupt you. The beginning of a book is a bit confusing to think about, especially how you should start it and what you should write about. If you're like me, the TV will distract you the most.

So, my favorite place to write is at my local coffee shops. Even though they can be noisy, I am somehow able to tune out the conversation around me. I am always by myself, even in those busy places. It's not like people are trying to talk with you directly like they would at home. I also enjoy the local library because of all the books I see; it inspires me that so many other people have written stories, so why not me?

If you are going to do this, you have to make the time. Time is critical when it comes to writing a book. I am sure other authors feel the same way. I believe it's not as easy as one might think, and I have not been the one to put a spotlight on myself for it.

It wasn't that I did not have a lot of extra time; instead, it was the fact that I was single while I was writing this. This is really unusual for me because I have always either been in a relationship or married with a family. However, I happened to be single at the time I was writing this, so I had extra time to devote to making this book a reality. It's kind of funny because I kept telling myself all the time that I better hurry up and get this done so that I do not use it as an excuse to stay single.

During this time, I have been surrounding myself with anything that has to do with elevating the level of my life. Books and TV shows about great influential people, success stories, inspirational quotes, online motivational videos, and attending events to test the waters. I am changing myself and I see how it affects everything and everyone around me.

People are attracted to people of influence and that is how I want to spend the rest of my life. I can sense that some people are unsure how to take it all because it does appear that it is all about me.

I believe there are a lot of folks out there going through stages in their life where they may ask, "where do I go from here?" Or, "what should I do now?" This could be in your personal relationships, your professional career, a developmental stage, or life in general. For me, I am currently on a mission to become a key person of influence in my particular area of expertise, which is arranging paid meetings for business, people, and products. (I will discuss how I identified this as my area of expertise later on.)

When connecting business, people, and products, one thing I have learned is that hiring, maintaining, and training a business development professional is very expensive. The cost of having a startup business development representative set up a meeting has been measured with a cost between $500 and $600 per meeting. With the challenges facing new business owners to find, hire, train, and keep a good sales person or business development professional with sales lead cultivating experience, I think it makes perfect sense to focus my efforts on training Startup company founders and anyone else thinking about business development or sales on the skills it takes to do it yourself.

I have recently come to the conclusion that I've been specializing in connecting business, people, and products, and expanding the customer bases of businesses through arranged meetings using my own system and cultivated contacts. This system that I use saves you time, money, and frustration, and lowers your cost per meeting.

Let me ask you a couple questions: "Is there a business or person you want to connect with for your service? Do you have a product you want to launch or sell?" I can help because that's my specialty. I have the training and experience from years of cold calls, as well as the follow-ups to ask for the meeting—and this is the most important part of the sales process.

Asking for the meeting is the same thing as early closing skills. As we go through the chapters, you will also learn more about my thoughts as a KPI (Key Person of Influence) in my niche and how I became effective at setting up meetings just by doing this thousands of times. We should think of cold calling as an art, because there is a system to it.

Say you're doing research on a business person, then you turn them into a prospect, ask for a meeting, then you go for the sale, etc. The beginning stage is what I am an expert at. Google shows the definition of an expert as "a person who has a comprehensive and authority knowledge of a skill in a particular area." Webster's Online defines an expert as "having or showing special skill or knowledge because of what you have been taught and what you have experienced."

Researcher K. Anders Ericsson argued that for someone to become an expert in their field, they need at least 10,000 hours of practice. I call an expert someone who is a KPI, or Key Person of Influence, in a particular niche. If you have not read the book "Key Person of Influence" yet, I recommend that you check it out. In the KPI book I read, the five steps to becoming a key influencer and capitalizing on what you already know are outlined. Then the book goes through how to go from being a functional worker at a job to becoming a vital entrepreneur and creating something on your own.

My second reason for writing this book—and honestly I should have listed it as my first—is to leave a legacy for my daughter, Lauren. Earlier I dedicated this book to her, as well as to my stepsons Nathaniel and Alekzander. Unfortunately, I have missed a large portion of my daughter's teenage life, and she is now becoming a young adult and so are the boys.

They had to move away to live with their mother after our divorce. Lauren was 13 at the time and now she is 19 years old. She will be close to 20 by the time this book is composed, while the boys are now around 21 and 23. I want to surprise them: "so here is what dad has been up to." I hope it gives them some encouragement that you can do anything you set your mind to doing.

It's a tough deal not seeing your daughter on a daily basis as she grows up into her teens. We have stayed in touch throughout the years, especially on special occasions and holidays, and then there is the famous communications via texting. It's very hard to endure missing the actual time together, and it's not easy to explain what it's like to miss out. I want her to know I love her.

I am also thinking of my other close friends when writing this. I want to inspire a few of them to write a book or to work on achieving whatever it is they want and to focus on their profiles as they move forward in life and in business. I believe publishing a book is the way to go about it.

I also want to mention a close friend who has been in my life now for over three years. I think her life would make a great book as she has a great story to tell as a single mother making her way through college, building a career, and raising kids. She pulls it off in a miraculous fashion, and has done a great job. She has an amazing passion for wanting to give back.

I've told her many times that I hope she writes a book someday: hint, hint. (I know she will read this.) I feel that if someone has a compelling story to tell, it may help others. I believe it's worth it. She is an amazing person and has been influential in my life.

As for our relationship, we have both encountered our setbacks; we are both set in our ways. I am sure there are a lot of readers out there who can understand and know what I am talking about, especially those at my age who understand that time is so valuable. Believe me, I miss the support that comes with a relationship with her, and I also miss my family.

Although I am a semi-private person, I think everyone should know I am a normal human being. I have my own trials and tribulations just like all of you. But I have found that authors of some of the best books give details on their life to help readers get to know them. Just like them, I am certainly not perfect.

It does seem that the more and more I focus on raising the bar for myself; my circle feels like it is getting smaller. I can sense that some people may perceive me as becoming arrogant or full of myself, but it's just a matter of fact that I am on a mission to become more influential, and to give back as much as I can. I want to do this for myself before my time runs out. I hope I'm not viewed as selfish. Instead, I hope what I am doing is viewed as an accomplishment and milestone in my life.

I do not want to look back and wish I had written a book or focused my career going forward as a KPI before it's too late. I cannot stress enough how I feel that time is so valuable to me these days, and I know that it will not come back around, just like the character portrayed by the actor Will Smith knew in the movie, "The Pursuit of Happiness." The movie portrays Smith as a homeless salesman with a son trying to improve their situation. There is a scene where he is struggling in life and at work; he is not making any money because, in order to get his dream job, he has to start out as an Intern. One day, he decides to take his son to play basketball for some father and son time. He starts to tell the boy that he will never be good at playing basketball because he's not great (as the scene shows him throwing a shot at the basketball hoop and missing). He starts to tell his son he will probably never be good at it because it's not in your genes. But then all of a sudden he catches himself and says instead:

"Don't ever let somebody tell you can't do something, not even me. If you have a dream, you have to protect it. People can't do something themselves, they want to tell you can't do it. If you want something, go get it. Period."

I hope this inspires my friends and family, too. You all know who you are. I just want to remind all of you again this is dedicated to you. I hope all of my readers gain some additional insight on me. Maybe you will strive for something you have always wanted to do and not put it off, or maybe you just needed the inspiration from someone else like I did.

JOHN MCKEE

INTRODUCTION

This book is about making a decision to record parts of my career, leave a documentary, and show how I'm being schooled as I go through life so that I can eventually focus myself to become a key influencer. I want to create a new thought process in the world of business sales development and share the ups and downs in my life. I truly believe you have to publish what you're good at in some shape or form—blogging, writing a publication, or writing a book—while including stories about your life.

I am going to cover several things, and it will seem like the book goes back and forth in time and with subjects, just like in a movie. However, it actually makes sense to me to go back and forth in time because it's easier to understand how things may relate and have an effect on outcomes.

For example, three and a half years ago I had no idea I would be getting so much attention today, start writing a book in January of 2016, or even learning how to elevate my profile from experiences. I recently have had the pleasure of being seen in magazines, on local news, meeting big stars, or exhibiting at the largest tradeshows in America, all because I wanted to help a friend at work protect her fingers from injuries caused by using shears.

I created and patented a cut-resistant finger glove called *Cosmo Finger Guard,* and because of that I have met key people of influence. They have inspired me to realize what I have really accomplished and to harness it all.

This book is not about showing you step-by-step instructions on how to become a key influencer, because you can read that book yourself. And it's not how to become great at sales. But I will give some tips throughout the book on things you may relate to, experiences you may be encountering, and signs to look for that you may be a key influencer yourself.

I want to state that I am not special; I am just obsessed with the idea of raising my profile based on what I already know and to help others along the way. To that end, you will learn how I am good at connecting people, business, and products. I will give quotes from successful entrepreneurs. I'll also tell you there was no formula for what I did in my life leading up to this point. I did not have a road map or guide until now.

Later in the book, I will list the five steps on how to generate sales appointments on your own using the procedures I use. That's my niche, and that's what I've known despite all the different routes I have taken. It's all related somehow. I've been repeating that in business development and sales, nothing happens until you set the meeting.

If you are in sales, you can use the five steps to acquire more leads and appointments, or use it to showcase your selling techniques to set up meetings, which I believe is a great business model. These techniques can be translated into meeting anyone in business without becoming a stalker or a pest. It's the system I still use today in business development and I have fine-tuned it for today's social selling methods.

Now, I don't want to assume that the majority of my readers are in sales or business development, but if you are, there is an added benefit to having a copy of this book.

It was a very long road to get where I am today. I think about everyone else enjoying life while I spent a lot of nights writing; and trust me, I had a lot of temptation to just give up. I am also burying myself in studying other successful entrepreneurs, how to build a business and a brand so that it also elevates me. It is all best summarized in a video made by Patrick Bet-David, "The Life of an Entrepreneur in 90 Seconds." Look it up on YouTube and watch it, because that is my life right now.

So what makes me an expert at connecting business, people, and products you may ask? First, it's because I have the desire to go forward with it and by stating that I am puts me in a spot where I have to be what I say I am. But more important is my experience. I have been researching sales leads and arranging meetings for companies for over 25 years now, and accredit myself to making over 25,000 sales calls in one shape, form, or fashion; from in-person face-to-face meetings to phone, conference, cold calls or emails.

In the process, I have created and tested my own system. I learned from repetitive sales call approaches and setting meetings over and over. Although I have been arranging sales meetings throughout my life, I have had the opportunity to specifically focus on and test it now for the last seven years.

I published my first copy of my techniques in 2011, soon started talking about it, and then had my first presentation on the lead generating system at a women's leadership summit that was hosted by my friend, Doris. Now, many years later, I was recently invited to do a workshop for Score Mentors, a nationwide group of business volunteer leaders who help small businesses by offering free business advice.

I have made updates and modifications to the techniques in keeping up with the digital era and advances in social selling. I gave out copies to business reps asking me what system I use, and it's the same publication I am offering you in this book. It's also available on my website, http://www.business453.com.

There is nothing too technical about it. It's just how I arrange and acquire my own leads, and it works; just ask any of the six companies I have been contracted by for the last seven years while at Prairie Technology Alliance. They are all listed on my LinkedIn profile, so please feel free to reach out and connect with me there.

It's been fun and has finally led me to believe I can transform my life and knowledge by re-thinking the sales approach and writing this book. For everyone else, it's a life story and journey I think you will find interesting.

I have this idea about focusing on supporting and helping Entrepreneurs and Startups with training on various aspects of arranging prospective customer meetings.. It seems to me after attending dozens of Startup presentations that there is little focus on cold calling. This will work especially well for beginners and new startups who absolutely need to focus on sales leads and those who cannot afford a full time representative and need the training themselves.

I also plan on writing additional training material to cover a wide variety of topics such as Networking, Cold Calling, Arranging Meetings and Social Selling. Watch for them along with many other topics in the months to come. Everything will be available on www.business453.com

1 MY WORK HISTORY

When you purchased this book, the first thing you may have thought is, "What can I learn from this guy?" Anyone who knows me probably thought, well maybe it could be interesting. If you are in business development or sales, you may be wondering how does arranging meetings become a specialty or niche? What is connecting people, businesses, and products all about? What is so interesting about his life? I will answer all of these questions in this book.

First, I'm going to start at the current time in my life and will work my way back. I hope that if the business aspect of this doesn't interest you that my life journey may. I have some pretty interesting work stories. For example, while I am writing this book, I've hit a huge milestone in my life. It has triggered a light bulb moment and I am realizing that I need to be taking full advantage of this opportunity.

The opportunity is that I have recently been selected to enter into a strategic partnership with Https://asseenontv.pro/, which is owned by the Original Shark from Shark Tank, Kevin Harrington, and the inventor of the Infomercial and DRTV. Direct Response TV came out of the blue and it is so cool because we will be airing our Cosmo Glove on national and regional TV. I had the opportunity to meet Kevin for a brief chat and to do a photo shoot. Later in the book, I will give all of the details and discuss the process I went through from spending a large portion of my career in business development to where I am today.

Out of the blue, I developed a product because I wanted to help someone. All of this happened while I was still in business development connecting people, business, and products. The *Cosmo Glove* is an ideal solution to a problem that was going unresolved, and 33 months later I was awarded my first United States Patent. Now we are on to national and regional TV. It wasn't as easy as that and I will tell you more about the process later in the book.

For me the book is about a lot of things including that light bulb moment and my career chart going up and down and back and forth. It was definitely never in a straight line going straight up, and I am certain people must have thought I was crazy to invent a product. This whole thing triggered a process I may have never thought anything more about or written a book had I not invented a product, met Kevin Harrington, and then read his book on being a Key Person of Influence.

Because of everything that has happened, it has made me realize I already have a specific skill set. I've always known I have skills, but having gone through the process of inventing led me to read a book on how I could capitalize on business development, arranging meetings, and be the go to guy for that service. I have been in school the whole time: the school of life. Now, I can capitalize on my experience helping others, and so can you.

"But wait there is more!" Yes, that's a quote from AsSeenOnTV. I am not one who has ever wanted to say much about myself. I never have put much of a spotlight on me. I want to stand out from the crowd. Of course we all want to! But what is success? It is different for each and every one of us. So let's get started and dive into my journey. I hope that it may help you with your dream, whether it's a dream of creating a new product, starting a business, or leaving a boring job you hate. The job that you realize is making others more successful than you and is keeping you becoming your own key person is just around the corner if you look for it. Maybe you want to write a book. Maybe you want to find a way to give back and help others but to do it on your own. "We are all key people of influence".

Depending on what part of your career you are already in and whether you are just starting fresh out of college, or are like me and already spent a lifetime working in a specific field, creating and crafting skills in the real world will dictate how to go about what you want to do. It's the experience that will set you in motion, the repetitive things you do, the things that you do that make you happy, motivate you to get up and go. It's what you look forward to doing, and others recognize this too well.

I believe we have all been educated by experiences. You can get started anytime. It is never too late or too early. Maybe you have been a housewife all your life, raised children on your own, run a flower shop or a golf club, or maybe you have built a successful corporation. Let's not forget it's highly possible that you may just be good at your job. No matter what you are doing, there is a niche in it.

You can become the KPI in your area of expertise, but please do not just do it for money. It is amazing how many have to go to work just because they need the money. Sound familiar? When I examine myself and think about what I do every day, every week, I know I have to go out there and recruit new business and new sales opportunities. I am happy doing this and it doesn't seem like work to me—maybe it's because it's a very social job. No matter what it is, I just get up and go to work, do a good job, and work hard. I will share and examine a little bit about my past first so you can get to know me. What did I do to get here and where do I go next?

After high school, I went to college because that seemed the most logical thing to do. I still had no plans, and some of my friends moved away while others went to work at a factory because their parents worked there, or they knew someone who could get them a job. In any case, I still wanted to work, so I did.

I'll be honest, I never felt like I fit in at school or college. I admit I wasn't a model student, except in certain areas where I could be creative and use my own personal and natural skills. Why? Maybe it was the group of friends I had at the time or because I just wanted more out of life. Maybe I wanted to do something right away and I didn't feel productive sitting in class. I wanted to do things my way. Why do I have to conform with everyone else? Maybe I wanted more attention from everyone around me and at home. Maybe it was my way of being rebellious. Maybe I did not have the right mentors as a youth that I needed. Maybe I had zero plans of becoming a doctor, lawyer, or becoming the president a fortune 200 company. Maybe I felt I could never do anything like that.

As I look back, I am certain I was not tagged as the one who would be the most successful. I do believe that if your plans are to become a professor, doctor, or lawyer then you must stay in school and get the education that is needed to do the job well.

If you're good at selling, and you like new business ventures, are a good negotiator, love to talk a lot, view struggling as a challenge, like raising capital and love creating ideas from scratch, then becoming an entrepreneur may be for you. This makes me think of a really helpful video I recommend when you have a moment to watch it. It's a YouTube video on whether or not you should stay in college by Patrick-Bet David called *"Stay in School or Drop out of College?"* It's fairly new and current with all the reasons why you should or shouldn't stay in college. By all means, it's a requirement these days to have a college education. If you watch the video, you will get a better idea of what it is I am trying to say. He certainly does a better job of explaining it than I can. I will understand if you want to pause to check this out and come back.

By the way, all of the people I am mentioning in this book, like Patrick Bet-David, Grant Cardone, Kevin Harrington, Gary Vaynerchuckand Daymond John are all people I follow on social media to find inspiring information and to study their actions and methods for how they became successful. I listen to their advice. They have all been an indirect mentor to me and have reinforced that everything I have done up to this point in my niche, my own intellectual property, and how it can be branded. I suggest you find a mentor too, and I will talk a little bit more about this in a later chapter. Mentors are critical to my success, and I will point a few more out as we go through my job roles.

Another area that is big for me, is reading daily inspirational quotes. These help me get by each day: they are the first thing I send out in the morning and the first thing I read myself. I practice what I preach. Somehow, I have managed to send an inspirational business quote out each business day of the week for the last seven years. I am just now realizing how consistent I have been; even when I am on vacation, I will still research a quote and send it out.

Now, I am starting to push them out to the public with a variety of not only other people's quotes, but also some of my own. I am learning from my mentors to focus on what I like and what I am good at as a business. You likewise need to develop a system on your social media accounts to push out motivational writings. Just look at it as if you are in business for yourself, with you as the branded product. You can see some of my quotes on LinkedIn, Twitter, Facebook, and my website. It will help to give ideas of how to start your own motivational writings.

Speaking of those people that I look to as a mentor, I don't feel I had enough time with my parents to garner their support as mentors. This is not something I hold as a negative thought or hold a grudge against them at all.

Both of my parents worked hard and that part I remember very well. They also put me to work at an early age. They have both since passed away, my dad at an early stage in my life. I was around nine when he passed away, resulting in me only having small pockets of memories with him. I wish I had more time to spend with him. From what I remember, he was a Vietnam War Veteran, a welder, and a troubled guy. He did the best he could, but was in and out of VA Hospitals, likely from what he encountered during the war.

I really feel for the men and women who serve our nation today. I salute all of you. I have never served, but I saw the effects war had on my father, who also had cancer in his late

40s. He passed away at 46. It was really tough for me when I hit 46 myself, because though I still felt very young, I kept thinking of him. It seemed like that would have been such a quick life, because 46 years certainly went by fast, and now I am already 53. Rest in peace Gordon C. McKee.

When I look at his pictures from the military, I wonder what he was thinking. I must say he looked pretty darn good, and I am glad. It makes me happy to see him that way. As a civilian, I remember his working years were pretty tough as well. He was a welder at a coalmine company in Victoria, IL. I remember that he loved Clint Eastwood westerns and Looney Tunes cartoons, like the Road Runner and Tasmanian Devil.

My mother passed away when I was 31 years old so I was able to at least have her around for much of my life growing up. It was no cakewalk for her either because she lived alone after my dad passed away. I helped her as best I could with things around her home, errands, and yard work, and we enjoyed our time on small trips, shopping, and during holiday events. She even gave me my first car.

Quite some time after my dad passed away, she should have moved on with her life. She tried to. I remember that I didn't like any of the guys she met after my dad passed away. I guess I am confessing here that this certainly didn't help. It's sad to say and I regret it. I am just sharing in case you can relate to a similar situation of growing up in a single-parent home. I miss her.

Although she is resting in peace, I wish that she could still be here to give me advice on my life and my book. I wish I could talk with her about moving on and meeting someone. Unfortunately, I do remember in her final years she always said she did not want to be a burden. I image when we are much older and are alone, how that may feel to think about and to say that. She passed away with pancreatic cancer and it was horrible. I would never want to see anyone go through that again. It's a very tough memory.

2 IMPRESSIONABLE YEARS

Here is where I will start with my training, at work and in life. I believe in each topic I experienced, I have learned something just as if I sat in a class. Some I have passed and some others maybe not so much. It's all knowledge paid by time and lessons I learned by applying and doing.

I started to work in the 70s before I started high school. My first jobs were usually during the summer and included landscaping, working as a bottle boy at a grocery store, and canvassing for home improvement companies. I have learned a lot from other authors who have been successful. They tell similar stories about the simple jobs they had as they worked their way up in their careers. I learned that I am not the only one who had embarrassing jobs. The landscaping job I had was just summer work, and I enjoyed being outside working with plants, bushes, and trees. It even required a little bit of artistic work to arrange everything in order for it to look good. It was fun, but the three things I want to point out as takeaways were the hot weather, hard labor, and mean boss. My boss, for example, was so bad, he would make everyone feel like they were beneath him and to watch out or else he would fire you.

After completing the project I was working on for him, I left to go work on my own and I started mowing yards. I would go door-to-door looking for lawns that needed some attention and secured my own jobs. I would figure out that if it was a hot day, I could use that to talk homeowners into giving me the work so they could relax. Besides, it's not like I was expensive. There I was, out there setting up jobs way before I even knew that what I was really doing was cold calling, closing deals, and filling my sales funnel.

It's amazing because all of that came naturally to me, and at least I wasn't out getting into trouble. You just do not see that work ethic a lot anymore. I certainly did not have any training, and I wasn't taking anyone with me to handle the conversations at the door. But I do remember I had so much work stacked up, in essence becoming the neighborhood lawn boy, that some of my customers had credit with me and negotiated terms like, "I will pay you as soon as I can." Eventually I had to get my brother-in-law to help me collect my money.

Can you believe that, mowing a yard and not getting paid at age nine or ten and having to go do collections? Why would someone do that to a young kid? So, I quickly learned the value of my work, and how I might not be able to do it all on my own. I needed help with the collections side and past-due money, even with a task as small as mowing. You may not be able to do everything on your own because if you are successful, you will eventually need a team.

I remember setting up a meeting with my brother-in-law at ten years old to go with me to some of my clients' homes to collect the money owed to me. Isn't that hilarious? What would have been cool is if this was today with all the technology we have now. I would have probably had a business Lawn Maintenance page on Facebook or an Instagram showing my work. I could have used the Square on my phone to swipe credit cards after completing a job. It would have been cool to be able to market a business at ten.

After this job, I started working at a grocery store as a bottle boy. My job was to collect pop bottles customers would bring back empty for a refund or credit. My responsibility was to take the cart full of bottles to the back stockroom and stack them up. I was a good kid, kind of shy, and liked by most. To this day, I am still friends with a few people from the grocery store on Facebook.

I remember thinking how I would like to move up the ladder so that I could be a stock person. They seemed to have the cool jobs. I wanted to at least work my way up to work at the lanes and bag groceries.

But among all the memories I have of working at the grocery store, the one that stands out to me the most was the biggest scare of my life. This certainly taught me a very valuable lesson and that was having the police called on me by the store manager. Allow me to explain I was about 12 or 13 years old. One day I was stacking bottles, and I remember it was a very cold. The stockroom where you take the bottles wasn't heated very well and sometimes their back door would be opened for one reason or another. This made it even worse.

I was extra busy, and I remember my hands where freezing. I couldn't even pick up the crates to move them around. I saw a pair of gloves in the stock room and put them on. I just wanted to protect my hands to go outside to get the bottles and bring them in. As I look back, I am fascinated how I am once gain involved with a protective glove. I feel that this event relates to me somehow creating a protective glove later in life.

Anyway, the manager that hired me, who was also a friend of the family, called the police. I was under age and a juvenile; I remember a detective coming to the store during a busy part of the day and telling me I needed to come with him. I was blown away, scared as hell, and not even sure what the heck I had even done. I had no intentions of taking the gloves home at all. It never even crossed my mind. I just saw them laying there and put them on because I didn't have a pair.

They called my mother and she came to get me. I was sent home with her, and I was not arrested because of my age. Man what an ordeal and how embarrassing. It's bad, and its good I guess; I learned early on to not take anything for granted or assume anything even though I just wanted protection. I just didn't know enough about life to realize what I was doing. I wasn't hurting for anything and certainly wasn't trying to steal. My hands were too cold to do the job I was asked to do. My lesson was learned.

However, shame on them for not offering me the correct protective hand attire. They didn't ask the butchers in the cold room to wear a tank top and sandals. They all had the proper protective gear, so why shouldn't I have the same? I don't know if it has any relation to me later on inventing a specialty glove.

It is kind of ironic and helped me see the value in personal protective equipment, which I offer today. I have the desire to help others. I have not been in trouble like that throughout my life since. The moral here is to ask permission; do not assume. Be prepared and be honest, even as a kid. No excuses. You have to work for what you receive. I am learning the hard way.

I remember being sent out to work in another cold environment. My parents told me one day that I now had a new job delivering newspapers. This was in the 70s in Victoria, IL. I started delivering newspapers in the dead of winter. It wasn't that bad and I did not take anyone's gloves, in case you're wondering.

From what I recall, the people of Victoria, IL were really nice to me. Most of them gave me gifts and tips for enduring the cold. I do believe they felt sorry for me.

It was my second experience at going door to door and receiving something in exchange for giving a service. My mom and dad evidently wanted me to learn to work at an early age and to stay busy and out of trouble, I guess. This tells me where I got my work ethic. Nothing was just given to me. I remember if we went to town for a hamburger at McDonald's, that was a huge event and very special. My family wasn't rich but mom and dad both worked.

My mom worked at a meatpacking facility in Victoria, IL, where one day she cut part of her thumb off slicing meat. As she was running a slab of meat across one of the meat cutters, she chopped off the tip of her thumb and evidently did not have access to the proper PPE (personal protective equipment), in this case a cut resistant glove. Or maybe they had it available and she chose not to wear it, but as she pushed the meat through the blade she caught her thumb and took the tip clean off.

What does this have to do with anything? Well this event probably did have a lasting memory on me. As a child, I didn't think anything at all about where her protective glove was. I do remember her having her hand sewn to her belly to heal and, at the time, that was probably the latest in surgical techniques. Later in life, I did create a safety glove, but we will get to that later.

My dad worked at a strip mine digging coal; he was a welder by trade. I recall all kinds of PPE laying around in the shed—helmet, gloves, apron, etc.—all gear he needed to protect himself while welding on the job. Both my parents were hardworking, blue collar Americans. I never heard much about his experience in the military. I just saw pictures. My parents kept it pretty quiet. I know we had to do a lot of traveling and a few fun trips with added sightseeing. My relationship with my dad was almost nonexistent from what I can remember. The things that stand out the most were, as I mentioned earlier, that he loved Clint Eastwood Westerns and his ability to be funny and sarcastic. He had a Tasmanian devil stuffed animal; you know the one from Looney Tunes cartoons that used to chase the Road Runner and could never catch him. I ended up with the Tasmanian devil after he died. The other big thing I remember was one Christmas he was expecting a bonus from work and I think he got it because I remember for the first time our being able to go Christmas shopping. He asked me to point to all the things I would like to have. This was really cool and I remember I wanted a motocross bike. I didn't want a Mini Bike, which I did get later in my childhood as well as a go-cart. The bike was the first of its kind, with the fenders like a motorcycle. The cross handlebar and knobby tires were pretty cool, too, and I couldn't wait to try it out.

I had two older sisters who both still live in Galesburg, IL, Karen and Janet McKee. They are still close and we see each other on Facebook. They are very supportive of my product venture, my career, and me. They are always there cheering me on, and they do not realize how much I appreciate it. I should tell them more often. It makes me happy to know that they are proud of me.

My advice to anyone reading this is to please keep your family close, because you have no idea when they may not be there anymore. But it makes me happy that they are proud. I want everyone to know I was never doing any of this to get rich and famous. The legacy I want to leave is that you can do anything you want to do; just go for it.

So, in thinking about the early stages of my experiences so far, I see how I learned the value of the dollar by working hard at landscaping, building a lawn mowing business, and my very first cold calling experiences trying to get a meeting on the spot. I learned about having to collect my hard-earned dollars. I learned the value of other people's property by stacking pop bottles.

Working in the cold taught me the value of proper clothing and protection at a very early age. Right around that same time my mother was injured at work by slicing her thumb. All of these left major impressions on me. I remember writing that Snoopy book. All of these things that I learned and experienced fit in well with how to deal with people, relationships, the value of money, and the need for protective products. Nothing is free or handed to you.

3 IN YOUR FACE SALES TRAINING

My first real, true sales and entrepreneurial role under another authority was an opportunity to work as a canvasser for a local siding and home improvement company. I was connecting all three things here: people, business, and a product. What I remember the most during this time was watching my closer. A closer is a manager role. Once the meeting is set, they go in to close the deal. These guys are also my mentors. I looked up to them. This is also one of the jobs you could never forget.

Back then these guys where bold, very aggressive, and making a ton of cash. I liked it. Now, remember this is also a summer job. I admit I was driven by the money and attention. I can say I was the best canvasser out there because I had already done it a few times on my own. I am a seller of meetings.

I have to also admit that I am not proud of some of the deals we put together. Looking back, it's funny now. I use the stories from this job to lead in speaking engagements because they are my favorite and absolutely make the greatest impression on anyone listening. You will see why in a moment. I saw the true side of "Tin Men" just like the 1987 Hollywood movie. If you get a chance to watch it, check it out.

The movie was exactly what I was living. It is about a door-to-door aluminum-siding salesmen Bill "B.B." Babowsky (Richard Dreyfuss) and Ernest Tilley (Danny DeVito) who are professional rivals in an industry known for shady dealings and high-pressure sales. I was very impressionable at the time. I was caught up in the rush of the guys I worked around and the money. Honestly, I was also a bit intimidated.

We did some bad things to good people to make deals. Let me assure you, we never hurt anyone. At the end of the day we did improve home values. I am talking about hardcore closing techniques, the in your face sales. They will not leave your house or get out of your recliner until you sign the contract type of selling. Funny right? Do I have your attention?

Let me tell you it was like nothing I have ever seen or will see again. If you have ever been around that type of selling, I am not sure if it would be a good or bad thing. I tend to think it's just experience. This shows how time affects everything, including selling trends.

I often wonder where the guys I worked for are at now. Since I am 53, they must be in their seventies or older. Let me tell you though, these guys where shrewd, tough businessmen. They would have a quick drink after work, party, and live to make deals again the next day. Cash was king. If you're not on the sales board back at the office you better kick it into a higher gear. Every closer wanted to have their own canvasser and they would recruit you in line at McDonalds. After some brief training, they would take me to neighborhoods and some were out-of-town neighborhoods I had never been to before, drop me off, and leave me.

Can you believe it? I was barely able to get a work permit. Back in those days you needed one to go door-to-door. It's possible you still need one today in some areas.

My job was to go door-to-door for hours carrying brochures knocking on eventually hundreds of doors to try to set appointments to make the connection for the closers. I would set their appointments so they could give free estimates. The closers have one thing in mind and that is to get the business on the spot.

What they really wanted to do is present a new siding solution versus painting and to try and sell it on the spot. In those days everyone still painted their house; siding was revolutionary and those who sold it had very high profit margins. I remember I was pretty good at setting up meetings. I was free to do as I wanted, knock on as many or as few doors as I wished, and make a lot of easy money at an early age—more than my friends did anyway. I did not know at the time that I was an entrepreneur. I was in high school and I had a ton of cash and could now buy a sports car if I wanted to, so of course I did.

My first one was a Trans Am from the Smokey and the Bandit era. With that came attention and girlfriends. Maybe this is where it started. I remember even getting a small travel trailer on a deal my boss made from one of my meetings. The customer couldn't afford the siding so he did a deal that was part cash and part trade involving a real nice travel trailer he had sitting out back. So when my boss sold the deal, he gave me his older mobile trailer in exchange for a commission, and I couldn't even drive yet and didn't even have a driver's license.

Can you imagine your teenager coming home and you asking how their day went, and their reply is: "I was paid by receiving a travel trailer today." I ended up having my boss take it to one of the local travel parks and we put it there. So that summer, guess where I would be hanging out? My friends thought it was a cool hangout when other teenagers just had an old rickety fort.

Of course, back then I was paid in cash and I wasn't thinking about a career in business development or in inventing anything. But I was learning how to be a creative thinker and how to get a homeowner to open their door to let us come back and give a free estimate that ended up being an in-home sales pitch for siding, windows, and gutters. I'm a teenager in school, and I have the opportunity to learn what it's like to connect people, business, and products all together though the simple task of selling a meeting.

I am already responsible for setting up deals, and although the selling tactics used then are no longer acceptable now, it was how it was done: aggressive and in-your-face selling with a call to action on the spot. There is no tomorrow, no add on, or blue light specials; just buy now, and if you don't we will be staying for dinner.

Think about this sales tactic and if you could use it today. Imagine you're a new representative for a window company and your job is to generate leads for the closer who has the technical experience with replacement windows. You meet the homeowner at the door and you give your brief pitch about being in the area and already doing a job nearby—this is how it worked. You explain you are offering a free estimate on replacement windows and a few of their advantages and savings factors, and they agree to setting up a meeting with you for a later date.

I mean, what could be the harm, right? You seem like a nice young man and trustworthy. So, when your day is over, you discuss the leads you set for the next day. Now, you are ready to go back to the homeowner, and just before you go in, the closer says to you he has a plan. "So listen up. What I want to do is go in and start the meeting off with a brief introduction and then proceed to start measuring windows and write up the quote. And when I am done, I am going to try and close the deal on the spot. And if they are not interested, I am going to fire you." *"What? Fire me?"* "Yes, fire you in front of the homeowners.

"When they decline to buy, I am going to say you told me they were ready to purchase today, and when we find out that they are not ready and tell us we just wanted an estimate, I will proceed to give you a hard time in from of the homeowners and then send you to the car. I will tell them you are fired for not being truthful and wasting everyone's time." Imagine my being so young, and I have never had a real sales job for a company, and I feel like it sounds kind of rough, but I do not know any better, so I agree.

I mean this is my boss, and I am learning the job right. So right in front of the customer, he acts out being upset with me and apologizing to the homeowners that I wasted there time, and I said they were ready to buy. "Please go wait in the car," he tells me after rudely firing me and embarrassing the crap out of me. So I leave to go sit in the car.

Can you imagine the homeowners surprise, and before I leave the homeowners are able to get a few saddening words out. "Please do not fire this young man," they say with a big surprise. You could tell they felt horrible as I walk out. I go to the car and sit. I remember because it was a cold winter and I didn't have the keys. I remember sitting and waiting, wondering what the heck was going on in there. It seemed like an hour went by, and I am sure it was at least that.

My boss, the closer, finally comes out and gets in the car and tells me good job. *"What? What the heck do you mean,"* I ask? He says again, "Good job, I got the deal," and I am thinking, *"Holy cow!"* He explained to me that they felt so bad for me that they purchased the windows on the spot; he got a check for the down payment, signed the agreement and they asked him to please not let me go. He told me this was a closing technique, and he said this is how we do it.

Can you imagine doing that today at Lowes? Having your boss come up to help with the sale and then firing you as a closing tactic. You're probably laughing right now because I am. That was crazy, but that is how it was then, and that was my first real experience with matching people up with a business and a product.

Little did I know, I was good at it, and that deal made me three or four hundred dollars for an hour's worth of work arranging the meeting and then sitting in a car. Now multiply this over dozens and probably hundreds of doors. It was easy for me, and, yet, I was the low man on the totem pole, but I think I made more money than them because my time investment was a fraction of theirs.

It only takes me a few minutes at the door to get an appointment and them an hour or two to close it, and sometimes they have to come back several times. So you tell me, who had it made and who had the better job, after all? Nothing would have ever happened; had I not set the meeting, no sale would have ever been made. Which is why I feel we should focus more on selling the meeting versus having a high-salaried person do it. Let them focus on the closing.

I also remember going on a deal I arranged that just so happened to be a teacher of mine. I can remember being in their house and the deal is not going well. The closers are well past the demonstration and are now on to the close. The homeowners are not ready and want to think about it. On top of that, the man of the house is my schoolteacher, so I am sure that's partially how I got the appointment.

Anyway they are not ready and the guys I am with (the Closers) will not leave. They tell the homeowner we are not leaving because they know how bad the homeowner needs the improvements, so we will stay until we agree on a good deal. By now, they have taken over the guy's living room, and one of them is sitting in the guy's recliner with it all leaned back like he owns the place.

I hope this is painting a good picture for you. Can you believe this type of selling used to happen, and with a young kid like me, and it's just my summer job as a canvasser? I just didn't know any better, and I trusted my mentors to be doing the right thing. I mean, it didn't feel right, but I had never seen or worked with another company like this. Even though it seems harsh to me, I figure the guys are right; he needed siding or windows, and we were there to give him the best deal possible.

So what else did it teach me? First, it made me realize that I did not want to be the hard, pushy sales guy to customers, nor did I desire to be the closer because it was easier to just make the connection and still make the money. I was also learning about business sales and the freedom to be an entrepreneur. I watched the experts craft their perfect pitch and "wow" statement, then do what they do best, which was to improve your home's value, insulation factor, and save you time and energy—a long sales pitch if you ask me. Honestly, I had the easy part, and their job was hard in my opinion. It's funny because it was looked on as the closer having the cool job, but not to me. I learned the power of numbers and the more doors I knocked on, the more appointments I would set, and it became easy for me.

I was self-taught, and I was in charge of my own destiny. I had crafted my skill, and the meetings were all because of me. I set dozens of these meetings up and I made them possible. And, even though at the time my role was viewed as the worst job, they couldn't have made some of the deals possible without me.

I was a teenage sales broker, but yet the other closers all wanted me on *their* team. Even though they were tough guys and the sales tactics were off the charts, in the end we really did help people save money over the long run. I can say I have seen it all and lived in an era of real pitch men—good, bad, or indifferent—and I could go on telling you more stories about those days, but I 'm sure you get the idea.

Maybe my version should be a Hollywood movie, especially focusing on the kid. Maybe I'll get lucky and someone will read the story and want to hear more. Remember earlier I mentioned how this taught me about sales tactics? Think about it: I was responsible for setting it all up and connecting *People, Business and Products*.

4 BAD BOSSES CLASS

This area of my life reminds me of the 2011 Hollywood film "Horrible Bosses", a film directed by Seth Gordon. The plot is for the movie's stars to take out their overly aggressive and mean bosses. I have never thought of taking anyone out, but it's a funny movie that I can relate to from a comedic standpoint.

As I got past high school, I started college. I was taking computer classes at Carl Sandburg College and working at an undisclosed big box retail chain as a shoe clerk, stocking shelves, meeting customers, and trying to make my way up through the retail ranks. I have one bad memory while working at this store in Galesburg, IL, that I have to write about because it will probably shock you as much as it did me. Maybe someone will read this who will remember working there with me during the late 70s or early-80s when this happened.

This store was the real deal, there were no Walmarts or Kohls yet, nor even Amazon. I do not even remember Sears being around, so working there was a big deal. I think it was my last month working and the manager at that time was having an in-store promotion and a drawing giveaway for a sailboat.

I remember a huge two-person sailboat sitting right in the front entrance of the store where you walk-in with its sail fully upright brandishing the Quaker State logo. I remember thinking how cool it would be to win it, and someone *was* going to win that baby so it might as well be me. Since employees were allowed to enter the drawing, I did.

Well the day came around for the drawing, there was a large crowd and everyone was in anticipation of winning it. They drew a name and read it out loud. "And the winner is; John McKee!" Holy cow, I won! I have never won anything and I was the center of attention. I thought I hit the jackpot.

I had a small pull-around travel trailer and now a sailboat and, boy, was I am happy camper, no pun intended. The downer bad boss moment that stands clear in my mind to this day, like it was yesterday, is coming up.

Imagine all of the focus is on me and there is a large crowd on hand because everyone wanted to win it. The store manager comes over to hand me the winning ticket and just when I thought I was going to be given a real quick congratulations speech and pat on the back, he instead leans in towards me and quietly says, where no one else can hear him, "here you go, enjoy it, because it's probably the only thing you will ever win in your life."

Boom! He lets me have it. I have no idea to this day why he would say such a thing, nor did I pursue trying to find out why. In fact, I have never said anything about it until now because it would have been embarrassing to me. Plus, it would have turned into some big affair, and I was just a bee worker anyway.

But one thing is certain: I was a very good employee, always working hard, on time, social with customers, and able to get the job done, so maybe he was jealous. That was a very long time ago. I forgive him, anyway, but again it's one of those moments in time I will never forget.

Think about how young and impressionable I was:, looking up to mentors like him, just trying to earn a wage. It's this type of comment that will drive you to do what others say you cannot do. That is what I learned. I do remember thinking much later as I sat in the boat on a lake, "what an asshole." But I would never have told him that out of fear of being fired.

It just blows my mind and, to some degree, it may have been a good thing, because I later wanted to prove him and anyone else wrong who had a negative impression of me. I remember taking that boat out to Lake Story in Galesburg, IL with a friend of mine and we sailed that baby with no experience. Heck, I did not even know how to swim at the time; I have never had lessons, and I cannot remember if I had my safety vest on or not. I wish I had pictures of us—that would be such a cool memory. I know how to swim today; I'm self-taught, but still not the best at it.

So the moral here is to set out to do the things that have never been done and ignore the negative comments from others, because they are just upset they cannot do it themselves. This has become the drive in me today.

Don't get me wrong, I met some great people there. The store seemed to produce some reputable people and a few were doing well at a young age. Now I am writing about it 35 years later. There is a quote by Maya Angelou, an African-American poet and actress, I want to share:

"People will forget what you said, people will forget what you did, but people will never forget how you made them feel."

So, for this experience I learned the power of wanting to prove someone else wrong. Not because they are wrong, but because there is something in each one of us that strives to do what others say we cannot do, just like the message I gleaned from the Will Smith movie. And in a positive way, winning the sailboat allowed me to become friends with a neighbor who I may not have connected with otherwise.

He happened to see the sailboat out in my yard and came over to check it out. From there we became fast friends and started sailing the boat together. I eventually sold it along with the portable pull-behind camper, since I was still not old enough to drive and would always have to ask someone to haul it. I did end up advertising both for sale and had no problems getting a buyer for either. That ended that era. My lesson or experience here is to be respectful to everyone, especially as a mentor in an authority role. Here is one more quote by Jimmy Dean:

"I can't change the direction of the wind, but I can adjust my sails to always reach my destination."

5 SMOOTH TALKERS CLASS

Soon after this experience, I remember being recruited by another new big box electronics store. At that time, it was the only electronics superstore. When I first came on board, I saw sales reps selling to one customer after another and making a lot of money. Despite my never having been in this type of retail atmosphere before, I thought it was pretty cool.

The methods these reps used started to rub off on me. The managers needed closers and wanted quick turnover because the walk-in traffic was high. I was being trained and mentored by these fast pace reps and it really interested me. So I applied what I learned on how to lead a customer through the buying process and soon became one of the power players on the team.

Now I was making good money, enough to purchase a car, and I bought a new Trans Am Camaro, with the new body style and T-Tops. It was such a neat sports car—the same style car that was in the Smokey and the Bandits Movie—and that made me feel pretty good.

This was a different environment than the cold calling of a door-to-door salesman or selling shoes at a department store. The sales process was pretty specific and they had a system that was almost like we would attack the customers when they walk-in—well not literally, but you know what I mean. We have all seen the type where you can tell they are about to pounce on you when you're shopping, almost like a shark preying on food.

I mean no sooner than you would walk-in than we had you, and the only other choice would be to turn around and leave. We would welcome you to the store, but we all kind of had attitudes because that's how we were trained. And believe me, if you didn't have that attitude of sell or be sold, the management would write you up and say you're not doing the job you are hired to do. Remember, we are still in this earlier era when there was not a lot of focus on customer enjoyment or satisfaction.

We would take the customer through the steps to make a decision today and buy now, so if you were just browsing you were in the wrong store. We would help you make a decision right now. When you think about it, it's not much different than the home improvement stories I shared earlier. And I'm sure you remember me saying I went along because that's what everyone was doing and how we were trained.

This was definitely the era of high-pressure selling and everyone was doing it. It did not mean that I had to be rude—I wasn't—but it was do or die. In time I did well and always hit my quotas and targets, and that allowed me to work my way up through the ranks from a top, competitive selling sales representative to assistant store manager, and then, later on, I was promoted to Store Manager.

As a manager, I had to act like a boss, and I learned how to teach others how to sell, sell, sell. We didn't force people to buy, and if the reps did, then all I had to do was talk with the customers and apologize. So I got to be the schmoozer, I guess.

This was a very long time ago, but I still remember the sales tactics. We were being trained to sell a certain way and close the deal on the spot. Make no mistake, we were good at it. This was way before social media and websites, and it was all about newspapers, bill boards, and radio advertising. It helped that we are the new, big box electronics store in town, so some of it was the right place at the right time, and this was the era we lived in.

Customer satisfaction was not what it is today. Back then, it was sell the customer, sell them more than they need, and if they didn't have the money we would finance it for you with a down payment. With financing came extra things you did not probably want, like adding a microwave or a VCR. Or how about a VCR cleaning package? When you're VCR heads are dirty, we clean them for you. Oh, and let's add an extended warranty for just a few dollars more.

You get the idea. We packed as much into the sales as we could. We were so good, we could qualify you for in store credit just by having a conversation with you without you even knowing we were qualifying you for a payment plan. Most customers thought we were just being friendly and being helpful, and to some degree, yes, we were, but everything we did was about making a commission and hitting our targets.

I remember having a manager who arrived in Illinois from Florida who hated Illinois. He called it "Corn Cobb America." I hope he is reading this because I know he would get a kick out of it. He would be so mean to customers, that he even caused two customers to fight. He was the type of guy that if you asked him to see an item behind the glass counter, he would reply by saying, "I don't know what you mean by asking if you can see it. Oh, you mean you want to hold it?" I have to admit it was so funny to watch him mess with customers.

He would call the late afternoon customers tire kickers or tooth pickers. You know the crowd that comes in after dinner with a full belly and is just killing time before going to a late movie at the theater. We could spot you from a mile away, and in our mind, we felt like it was a waste of our time to try and help, because we knew you are just browsing. Usually, the dead give a way was the toothpick in your mouth. They had no intentions of buying anything, and honestly, most of the time he was right; it taught me to qualify customers early.

In selling there is an old term called "stroked." Stroked is what happens to a salesperson when you spend a bunch of time with a customer and give them the full sales pitch, only to hear at the end they want to think about it. "OK thank you for your time, I am just browsing." Or, "I am shopping around." So all of the sales reps would tell each other while laughing out loud that you just got stroked. I was a game and it was funny, but not funny if it happened to you. But I got to the point where you know if they are buyers or not.

Then there was the "Watt Heads". These are customers, usually the younger generation, who would come in the store to check out the sound

room full of Hi-Fi Stereo Systems, big tower speakers, equalizers, amps—you name it, we had it. It was the first of its kind.

You remember those days. We had a closed off room where you could jam out and not interfere with our other customers. Now, you can buy speakers the size of a small carton of lunch milk and they pack a punch. Back then they were 5 feet tall and weighed 75 pounds.

We had names for all of our customers and they usually matched. The famous "watt head" are the ones wanting to crank up the car stereo to see how many watts it had. They always asked how many watts does this car stereo or that car stereo have? We actually placed a sign above the car audio section that said, "Don't be a Watt Head." Can you imagine what our district manager thought of this?

We also used the sales tactic mentioned early when they asked if they could "see" a car stereo. We would always reply, "oh so you mean you want to hold it, because I know you can see it since we are looking at it together."

This was my sales training experience from my supervisor, who was the same person who would later promote me to assistant store manager, then, eventually, to store manager. So I evidently was turning into him. I would never operate with an attitude like that as a manager and never did again.

He and I would also get into arguments about it all. The hardcore home improvement closers, the grocery store manager who called the cops on me instead of offering me the proper work attire, the retail manager who evidently didn't think I would amount to anything, and now a manager from Florida who hated Illinois and customers.

Wow, what a line up, right? What do you think so far? Do you see a salesman in the making? I still have no idea what I want to do; I am just going through the motions of life and taking things one step at a time.

What I think now, looking back, is that I had training that you cannot get these days and that's why I think it's so great to write about it. Although in most cases I was thinking "this is crazy" and wanted no part of the tactics, but it did teach me a lot about customer service, selling, closing, being creative, and thinking outside the box, as well as not having a problem approaching people. It also really taught me how to read customers and, as the book shows on the outside cover, I learned a lot about how to connect people, business, and products together through meetings, and it made me feel good, no matter if the meeting was on the showroom sales floor or on a doorstep.

It wasn't about the actual selling of goods, it was about the connection and how it all ties together in a magical way and the feeling that I just made it all happen through my words and actions. What an era we lived in, and even though some of it sounded extremely harsh, it all makes me smile, and you have to appreciate the experiences—good, bad, or indifferent.

6 BUSINESS SALES

Things get better, and this isn't to say I was unhappy or anything like that. It's just that being able to look back and put it all in perspective, I know now that there were good times and bad times, and this is true with anyone. I was still not clear what I wanted to do in life, and it is still in the early 1990s after the electronics store, high school, and now taking more business and accounting classes. It's now the era of total quality management, or TQM, and I am now at Illinois Central College. At this time, I've landed a job with more stability, structure, and customer satisfaction in mind.

In fact it's now the beginning of the Six Sigma era, with flow charts, process improvement, and how to get things done better, faster, with higher qualities, and some real potential to get serious business-to-business training.

The business world is always evolving, and we always hear that every two or three years this huge change will happen. The idea of a quick and easy sale is losing traction in a world that is now focusing on better customer satisfaction and efforts to get it right the first time with zero defects.

I am now working indirectly with a Fortune 500 giant, Motorola Communications, through the dealer channel with a company called Supreme Radio Communications located in Peoria Heights, IL and which is still in operation today. I have to mention the owner, Dale, because he may not know that I viewed him as one of the most valuable mentors I have ever had. Thank you Dale.

In fact, he was the first true entrepreneur mentor I had the chance to work with. And I got some of the best training from a small business owner here and at Motorola University. I am now designing and selling Motorola 2-Way Communication Systems that require serious technical knowhow, and this will also soon be my first attempt as an innovator.

I was already good with cold calling and now had to build customer relationships, solution selling, and value-added service to the business, and I was about to embark on big ticket selling. This part of my life runs for seven years and was my true developmental time. Not only did I develop during this part of my career, but I also met my first wife. I was with her for 13 years and now have my beautiful daughter Lauren, who I mentioned earlier.

7 WANTING MORE

It was during this period of time that I began to see what running a business of your own is really like. I was challenged to go out and find new customers and match them up to our products on a larger scale, which now means I have to get really creative and separate myself from other communication dealers and get the appointments set. For the first time, I am now using additional communications sources such as the phone, email, newsletters, and cold calls.

I did very well and set hundreds of meetings and became a number one salesman, winning several sales hero contests, sales trips, bonuses, and much more. Motorola even introduced a debit card that for every 2-way device I sold, I would equal dollars per $10 spent by the client deposited into a Visa debit card. That was the best incentive I've seen up to this point and it was enough to buy whatever I was in need of or to go anyplace I wanted. I remember coming home to my Peoria, IL apartment in my company car and my neighbor across the hall asking me if I just won the lottery or something because outside of my door there would be boxes stacked up in the hall from UPS delivering a new couch set, TVs, microwaves, furniture, and whatever I decided I wanted to order. This was all from the program incentive Motorola had for sales people.

Eventually I wanted to be more successful and I was not happy with just hitting my quotas and selling locally. I started reaching out further beyond the local businesses of Peoria. I had the knowledge and experience to connect anyone with our business and product. This was when companies like Menard's and Kohl's department stores started to build out all over the United States, and I knew they would need two-way communications in their stores for improved operations efficiency and security, so I started to approach both of them.

My training during this time not only came from Motorola University, but it also included Dale Carnegie Sales courses, Stephen Shiffman, and many more, which I will talk more about later.

I've learned that the more people I reach, the better my chances would be to increase sales, and I am certainly not afraid to ask for business. I love making those connections. Hearing a prospect say "yes" and hearing them say "I will talk or meet with you" is just a great feeling of accomplishment.

Most sales people get excited about the sale and that makes sense, but I like making the connection, and the sales will not happen until a meeting is set.

The first business on my radar was a large corporate level home improvement company and retail chain. I was able to get their attention over time with repetitive calls, shipping out free demonstration equipment, and following up; all the things that I learned to eventually put together in my own lead system.

I suppose I wore them down, and they saw the advantages of 2-way communications. This is at a time before cellular was available, or if it was available, it was too expensive. We also distributed satellite phones and they cost $10 a minutes to make a call, and you had better not be under an overpass because you would lose the signal.

I eventually got my satellite phone certification, but again it just cost way too much and was not cost-effective unless you were traveling to another remote country. But we had it, and it was so large that it was the size of a suite case, and the antenna on the car looked like a dome.

The home improvement giant eventually took me up on the offer to purchase from me. They sent a purchase order for about 300 2-way Radios, the largest order they had ever had. I was shocked and so was my boss. I did it; I bagged the big elephant.

But wait, not too fast here. This was also the first time I was really let down. To this very day, I don't know why they changed their minds, but they did. They canceled the order before I could fill it. Supreme Radio probably still has a copy of the purchase order as a reminder.

It was so frustrating, and I was so let down by all that work only to get a valuable lesson in business. That, my friends, is why sales is such a rollercoaster. So if you are married to a sales representative or dating one, and he or she seems beat up, you can remember my story.

Of course, it is not always like that, as you have already heard me talk about all the good times in sales, and those are okay—but this is large orders and system sales. These take time, and a lot of customer romancing. For me, I always have had other opportunities and good solid leads in my pipeline. It gets better, just like in the Hollywood movie, *Glengarry Glen Ross*. The story is where an office full of New York City real estate salesmen are given the news that all but the top two will be fired at the end of the week. The atmosphere begins to heat up quickly. Shelley Levene (Jack Lemmon), who has a sick daughter, does everything in his power to get better leads from his boss when he could have cultivated his own. That movie is great and I've seen it many times, but I am always amazed at the sales reps that depend on the house to supply leads.

I was going through the same sales process with several other large retail chains, and this was before others were trying. I felt like I was the innovator and to either go big or go home in my division. There was another really large department store working with me on the same type of communications systems. This company is the leader in department stores today and is still one of the fastest growing department store chains in the world. I took endless amounts of sales calls, phone calls, demo equipment offers, and deep-discount offers to get the meeting.

This one paid off, and to make a long story short, I landed this account, and this time no one cancelled. After a lot of hard work, dedication, and a "do not give up" attitude, I was now the official communications representative for this corporation nationwide. Not only was I responsible for the design and installation of equipment for their new stores as they built out, they also started building distribution centers, and I was the go to guy for those as well.

This was my largest account and I was very proud of it. I felt like the king of the world at the time and was certainly catching the eye of Motorola and other distributors. The systems we installed were becoming the standard communication choice for all the locations to come. This was the crème de la crème, and everything I had ever done led me to this apex point as a sales person.

This is one of the many reasons I now call myself an expert in arranging meetings. I know I am not the only guy in the world who can make a big sale, and I am sure there are deals happening all the time, but up to the point of getting this job,

I was self-taught.

Imagine the knowledge back selling lawn deals at nine and ten years of age. It's funny to think about what could have been then with today's knowledge. This is now the beginning of teaching me to work hard, think big, be resilient, and not give up.

It was teaching me lessons in life and building up my confidence. Before I end this portion about my Motorola career, I have to explain further because there is a lot more to it than just selling 2-way Communications systems. I wanted to invent something, and inventing led me to realize I could do much more: inventing led me to read *How to Become a Key Influencer.*

A lot of people may not know this, but Motorola was on the cutting edge of new development in areas of messaging. In addition to being number one on the planet with paging systems, Motorola was embarking on wireless Alpha Displays, which are large-format LED Moving Message Signs that could be controlled remotely and wirelessly. These types of LED signs were being sold nationwide from Sam's Clubs to small businesses, which could now display them in their store windows with programmed messages that announced they were open or having a sale.

Motorola made them available to dealers, and I wanted to do something big with them. I started researching the LED technology and found other manufacturers and distributors who we could buy larger displays from. And remember this was back in the mid 90s. Do you see a pattern in me yet? I was never satisfied with what I had to offer. I always wanted to go to a new level and innovate, and it seems that I have always wanted to be a KPI, but I just did not know how to harness it into step-by-step actions and go public. So I approached the owner of Supreme Radio Communications, Dale, about adding a new sign division to his company.

This was my first real investor pitch, but I did not know it at the time. It just came to me naturally. Although I wasn't asking for money to open a new company, I was asking that he take a chance on my idea and trust me. The idea of adding new products—which would ultimately cost him because he would need to buy inventory—was a risky pitch for me.

I think he allowed me to take this risk for two reasons. I was a top salesman there, and he became a believer in my mind. Let me explain a bit further. I remember one day, I was discussing my sales funnel, and I had one particular account listed that did not seem to be going anywhere. So, I told Dale I had an idea. I know how to get this company into a new, modern 800MHZ Trunked 2-way Communication System from an old out dated 150MHZ VHF system. I told him I would set up an appointment and explain how I am going sell the customer's 100-foot tower and their old communications system. Who in the world would be able to sell a tower bolted to concrete, used and weathered? It was unheard of. Who in the world is going to buy a 100-foot communication tower in Peoria, IL that is in the ground and would require deconstruction, a big crane, a large flatbed truck, and manpower? They would have to bring a tower crew to disassemble it and haul it away and then re-sell it, or reinstall it, someplace else.

He told me this sounds crazy, and it really did sound impossible. He actually laughed at the idea, plus most businesses could just go buy a new tower, as it would be a lot easier. You probably know how this one will end. Yes, I did my research and got resourceful, looking up companies in a local trade publication called *RCR Wireless News*. I found a company that buys towers and I contacted them and got the price they were willing to offer for the tower. I added that to my proposal on new equipment as a discount on trade-in, and, along with finding a buyer for their old radio system, was able to show it all as a trade-in on the new system. Bingo. I arranged the meetings, made a deal, and got the order. Dale was amazed.

So this is why I believe he trusted me to get things done by doing what others said could not be done. Doesn't that drive you and most of us? I did my due diligence to make things happen, went above and beyond what normal was, and took my own path. It shows how I was becoming the resourceful person I am, and in a way, inventing a new idea. I certainly did not know I would later invent anything. Looking back, I can now see how I was a creative thinker: a person who saw a problem or obstacle and could figure out a solution to get it done. This is my point here.

Let's get back to those Wireless LED Signs I was talking about. They still amazed me. I did my research to find bigger and larger sign manufacturers and distributors, and even got Dale's permission to let me expense trips to visit a few to get acquainted with their manufacturing processes and technologies. I was carving my own path here and not following anyone; this was my idea and great leaders lead the way.

After reviewing the LED manufacturers, I settled on a few that really caught my eye. We made a few sign purchases and started stocking demos, lining up a local sign company who could do the installation on some of them we sold, and used our wireless background to create a way to communicate the messages via wireless connectivity. We did make sales and we were way ahead of our time for this type of technology, and honestly we should have filed patents. In fact, I remember presenting the idea to large billboard companies to use the LED technology to control billboards and revolutionize the outdoor advertising industry. I could absolutely see the vision, but no one would make the jump that large with me, yet today you see this all over. So it took 15-20 years for it to become common for businesses and advertising companies.

Now let me tell you another quick story about my brain on overload and my beginning as an idea man and not knowing it. I do not know what drives me but something inside of me wants more. I dream larger and I not satisfied with the norm. Because after seven years as a successful Motorola Communications Specialist, and after creating a new LED Sign division for the dealer from the inside, I now had a new vision I wanted to try on my own.

For seven years, I had been watching Dale run his company and I started thinking I wanted to do the same. I learned a lot while I was there, watching all the ups and downs. I watched him worry about making payroll from time to time, but I also watched him enjoy success as well. I was a sponge soaking it all up and I liked it. I now wanted to run my own business and I had an idea. I learned the value of the sales process, sharpened my selling skills, and now I wanted to hone in on opening new doors. And it all started with an idea and an appointment.

8 WINNING FRIENDS, INFLUENCING PEOPLE

One of the most important times in my career, I believe, is my training at Dale Carnegie College. While I was at Supreme Radio and Motorola, I had the privilege of attending several 12- to 16-week certified training programs, and we also had to read *How to Win Friends and Influence People, How to Stop Worrying and Start Living,* and *The 5 Great Rules of Selling.* These are tied into sales training programs on cold calling techniques, call preparation, setting the meeting, closing the sale, and the follow-up. All of which also prepares you to work on language, body movement, and the way you dress and look. These are all key factors for becoming a KPI: you must look and feel the part and do it with confidence.

I remember the training, including having to look at yourself in the mirror and talk while presenting a call-to-action or creating interest in what you have to offer. It was also helping me get out of any shell I was in or comfort zone I had.

We are all sales people, to one degree or another, and we all are selling something and asking for a meeting constantly. It doesn't have to be a product or service, it could be persuasive selling at home over what to cook or what to buy or what TV show to watch. We all do it every day and do not think anything about it. Isn't that interesting we do this without thinking about it and don't even realize it? We are the most important person to our self and learning how to influence others is natural. But imagine knowing how to take the steps that have been studied; that is what Dale Carnegie does for you.

I honestly cannot say I knew what I wanted at this point of my life and career. I look back and think to myself I believe that it was all planned to not plan, that life just happens and whatever is put in front of you, you take. This is not to say you should not use good judgment and make good choices, it all has to make sense. The Dale Carnegie courses and training are still available today, and 20 years later my facilitator in Peoria, IL and I have recently become reacquainted through sales workshop opportunities at Score Mentors Peoria. Recently, he wrote a nice endorsement for me on LinkedIn. So you just never know what life will present to you and the Dale Carnegie training was a vital part of how I am becoming a Key Person of Influence with my skills. It is perfect training and I hang my training certificates up high with all my other accomplishments so I can look at them daily.

9 STARTUP MODE AND FIRST PRODUCTS

It's now April 1997, and it's now time to embark on my first venture. Towards the end of my career at Motorola, after making hundreds and thousands of sales calls over the years, I am starting to get the feeling that I've had enough of working for someone else. I can do it myself. This is my fist venture to take on sales without doing it from inside another company, making them money, and growing their business. I want my own business.

So, I started planning. I wrote a business plan and I even used my own money to buy my own signs and modified them. At the time, I did not know much about IP (Intellectual Property), patents, and trademarks, and I probably should have hired an attorney and filed them. However, I just didn't know what I didn't know, and I may have gotten rich had I known better.

I created a company called Display Communications. The premise of my sign company was to locate and lease space in large walking-traffic areas, like inside shopping malls, and sell space where advertisers would be targeting that type of audience, especially shoppers and mall walkers. So, I purchased LED signs, had them installed into large metal boxes with back-lighting capability, and they had four spots that would hold x-ray type images—duratran or translucent vinyl—that allowed light to emit through them.

My signs also had timers in them, so that when one of the four images would light up the LED display a moving message would match the image with an appropriate message, pretty revolutionary, I think, for the late 90s. I contacted Simon Mall management and set appointments in three or their four locations, signed leases for wall space, and installed them in two malls.

I created a pricing model and pitch material, set up more appointments with local advertising agencies to present the idea, and sold ad space. They seemed to love the idea and were interested in marketing health information and messages from local hospitals to the elderly mall walkers. I was on my own with my first real company and first real customers, setting meetings for myself.

10 SUCCEED, FAIL, SUCCEED

I feel I am unknowingly creating a path to where I am today by being an inventor, which leads me to writing and forging my way down the path of becoming a KPI. All these things had to happen for me to get where I am. I did not see it that way then, and I have even told many people to this day that I never invented anything before the Cosmo Finger Guard. But that is actually not true.

I did invent. I had invented a way to sell more communication systems at Motorola. I invented a sign division within a company. And now I had created a new mall LED Messaging System, and I started forming a system for arranging meetings even though it was called selling. This went well for a while but it was also my first failure. I have heard that successful inventors do not succeed all the time. I think it was Shark Tank's Daymond John, inventor of Fubu Clothing, I once heard say:

"Successful inventors succeed, succeed, fail then succeed."

It's true; I had succeeded and now I will fail. But do you really fail when things do not go your way? In a business sense you probably do, but in growing knowledge you don't really fail because you learn some valuable lessons. And if you learn from your failures then you will succeed. There are many quotes out there on this topic, and the best one that stands out to me is by Tony Robbins: *"There are no failures, only outcomes—as long as I learn something, I'm succeeding."*

You probably want to know how I failed with the LED Sign business. Well, I failed because instead of taking the money I made on the first deals and reinvesting it in my company's operating capital, then taking the time to make sure I had future customers, I used the capital to buy new signs and secured more mall space. So I was now working on my third mall and it turned out to be too many locations, too soon, and not enough prospects in my pipeline to make all the locations profitable.

I did the first location correctly by having a client ready and lined up, but I did not replicate that procedure on the second and third location. To make a long story short, I bit off more than I could chew and ended up closing some time later. The malls kept the idea running for years, and I would tell people, "I started that" or "it was my idea." So if I can give any advice here it would be to get a mentor and partners to get advice on business growth, planning, and business strategies. I was the idealist, but I was not the financial planner for growth. I learned a lot on this venture and it will not be my last.

After tucking my tail between my legs and walking away, I thought, that's it for me. I need to go back and get a real job and stop playing around. "You have a family," I said to myself. I think this is how a lot of people feel after trying a venture on their own and others will definitely make you feel this way as well. Back then, and for a long time, an entrepreneur was considered to be lazy, unmotivated, and unemployed. At least that is what I remember. You would have been ashamed to say you were, so you tell people you own a business; it sounds much better. I think it's because some people would never try to create a company or a new product on their own. They haven't been around that type of environment and have been brought up in a society to do what everyone else is doing—go to college, get a real job, and start a career, ultimately to work for someone else and help them be successful. I am not downplaying career-minded professionals, because there are a lot of people who consider themselves an Intra-prenuer. I don't know if that has become an official word yet, but an Intra-prenuer is someone who invents their place of employment from within, like I did while at the Motorola Dealership creating a new LED sign division.

A lot of people do this, and others are just flat out successful beyond imagination working for small or large corporations, growing to amazing levels even through tough times. Earlier in this book I mentioned a friend who I have been dating off and on now for almost three years who has had success this way.

She is a dear friend and extremely successful gal who works for a Fortune 200 company, and I think she is a bestselling book and Intra-preneur waiting to happen when the time is right. At times, she has inspired me to do better, and I have looked up to her. Her early life was no cakewalk and she endured more obstacles than anyone I know in life, but somehow has miraculously marched through it all with little to no help and today is one of the most successful women I know. I have told her many times that there are people out there, especially women, who would be inspired to read a book on how she became successful when all the odds were stacked against her. I am keeping her last name confidential, but many who read this will know whom I am talking about.

However, what I am talking about is truly going out on your own and starting something by yourself, a true Startup. This is very risky, and for someone who has a lot tied to a career—

i.e., a certain standard of living, bills, and a lifestyle that was created because of the income they make—they would find it difficult to just leave and start a business or launch a new idea unless they are 100% certain you have a sure shot. I get that, and let's face it, if life is good, you're making a nice living, you are okay with your job, and enjoy it, then I say stick with it. Being an entrepreneur is not for everyone. You can still retire a lot better off than other people including inventors. Creating businesses, products, and meeting people is in my blood, and it is my destination to keep becoming a Key Person of Influence, but I didn't know this at the time and I did apply for a job.

11 LOST IN TIME

I took a few odd positions and even remember selling cars for a while at a local Galesburg dealership. I am not saying this because I consider selling cars a bad job; I just did it because I needed work. There are many auto dealerships that have amazing and successful employees. It just wasn't for me. So, I tried to find a way to make this work for me and I remember thinking to myself how would I make selling cars my own. I remember my mind going into work overload again and I did come up with a system that I would find appealing.

Of course, my idea at the dealership was nothing new, but I did not see anyone else trying to sell fleet vehicles to businesses and this required the use of my business-to-business skill sets and arranging meetings outside of the normal dealership walk-in hours.

That's what I wanted to do in my short time there, and I started planning how to match people with businesses and products (cars) and make it possible.

At a car dealership, they seem pretty open to your ideas because at the end of the day most are on commission and you are really kind of self-employed, but have a proven product people want. This may have changed since the 90s, because that was then and this is now. This job didn't last because I had other resumes already out there and my mind was completely off of starting a business or any new ideas needed to go out on my own again.

I was out of money, had a wife, kids, house, and bills—playing around was over. So this is one of those times you read about an entrepreneur falling down. I remember it like it was yesterday.

And believe me, I do not recommend staring out on your own while having a family unless you are certain you are financially capable and your significant other is on board, because I can honestly say that although I had the finances to do it, I am remorseful that I did not consult my wife and family before starting. I mean I did tell them, but I remember it being more of me telling her that this is what I am doing, and it's not a question open for approval. Lessons learned and I will tell everyone reading this please put family first. I was good at business sales and arranging meetings, and I was searching for success.

12 STAND OUT FROM THE CROWD

It is now March of 1998 and I eventually receive a call from Pitney Bowes, the industry leader of Mailing and Shipping equipment. I was obviously amazed and seriously happy, another real job with a real Fortune 500 company. I remember thinking, I wish they would hurry up and hire me. It was a long process and they were looking real hard for sales closers. I had a decent resume at the time, having worked for Motorola, and a proven and successful sales track record.

After an extensive interview process, I did get the job, and I have a lot to share about this company and my managers. I hope they read this book, because I contribute my additional drive for success, business development, and meeting skills to them as well.

All of these roles in my life contributed something. I keep saying I didn't know the knowledge was helping me in the long haul and it's true. I had no idea what I wanted to do other than get a job, and that I'm good at cold calling and setting meetings, even before the era of social selling.

However, I was hired, and it was a new exciting time for me. The training at Pitney Bowes was well known and probably still is today's as one of the best and most intense sales training organizations on the planet. I remember the entrepreneur coming out of me again and my mind going on overload.

By the way let me put this out there first regarding "Mind Overload." It's a quote from one of my indirect mentors from the Original Shark from Shark Tank, Mr. Kevin Harrington. You will hear him use this reference in many of his presentations; it's a statement I feel fits my description very well.

During my training at Pitney Bowes, I remember a session with a hiring instructor who had the ability to terminate staff and I remember her asking the group of new hires from our district— around 20 in all—who she would see at First Honors. First Honors is a sales leadership recognition event held by Pitney Bowes for new hires that achieved a certain level of sales success in the first 90 days of being released into their territories. I remember her asking the group, "Who will I see at Marco Island for First Honors?" and I raised my hand in a knee jerk reaction and with a bit of assertiveness and said, "I will see you there." Of course after saying it, I was a bit intimidated that I put myself into that situation because honestly I had no idea what I was getting myself into. I did not know the quotas or territories yet, and only had a small amount of product knowledge up to this point, and hadn't even had my training or even orientation yet.

But I wanted the attention and felt challenged buy the superiority of the group in that room. I looked around and I did not feel like I belonged there because they all looked sharp, professional, and as if they were already successful. Trust me, I was as well, but I think this was my first experience with seriously polished sales reps from all types of industries. So I stepped up by opening my mouth and telling everyone I will be at First Honors, and it challenged the whole group. At the end of the first ninety days of employment, sure enough I made First Honors, just like I said I would. I made as many sales calls as I could each day with 9, 11, 1 and 3pm meetings. I arranged more meetings than anyone else, and it felt great each time I walked into the district meetings and report my statistics and hear my numbers. I was becoming a First Honors candidate and I only saw three others among the twenty new hires at Marco Island. Looking back it makes me smile because I still have the company marketing publication Pitney Bowes put out on a monthly basis that featured successful sales representatives, new products, company news, success stories, and interviews of overachievers. I didn't know the publication even existed yet, so it was not like I said, I would be at First Honors just because I wanted my name and picture in it and it was my first real going-public image.

Now, I realize the value of personal branding because being in there was a shot of fame. I did it as a reaction to how I felt at that moment in time. It is an interesting fact because later in the job I was told by the hiring manager and District Director for Peoria, IL that he hired me not because of my sales experience and success at Motorola, but because I tried to go out on my own and start a business concept that had not been done before. That is how I got this job.

So sometimes when you hear a quote or a mentor tell you that you have to first state your success and state whether it will be true, especially when you state it in front of a group of peers. You say it and then you do it and live it.

Becoming an entrepreneur and having that experience impressed my new boss. He told me he felt that was what is was going to take to be successful at Pitney Bowes. There are companies out there that look for a variety of business development people and sales professionals, and then put them up against each other to create sales rivalries, and this was one of them.

I remember the manager seemed to be the Ivy League type. Very polished, nice car, obviously successful himself, and was the District Director of Peoria. To me, that seemed like success, and he acted like it. He was very direct but was kind and professional to me at all times, so I could tell he had different attitudes for each representative there. He knew how to handle the group and capture our attention with intensity.

In fact, there is one specific time that sticks with me about his style as a manager. What would happen today if your manager or boss received a call from a prospect who complained that you have been too aggressive on your follow-up attempts and that you call to often? Most likely you would get called into the office for a talk and set on a different track, right? Well my manager did get a call one time, and I did get called into the office to have a chat about my sales assertiveness, and this is how it went down.

"John, I received a call from one of your prospective clients who was upset about you calling and following up too much, and he requested that I deal with you and tell you to stop calling." When I asked how he replied, he told me that he said he was not going to apologize for my assertive behavior. He said he went on to explain to the prospect that his representatives are charged with serious monthly quotas to attain, and they are trained to get the business or else. If they don't, they will not have a job. *"And the fact that you are calling me tells me I made the right hiring choice and that John is out there working hard and is doing his job, and I'm happy you called. John hasn't said anything wrong, been offensive, or really done anything bad; it's just him trying to get your business and arrange a meeting."*

My boss also went on to tell me that he asked the prospect if he could ask him a question? The prospect replied with "well,

I guess, go ahead." He then proceeded to ask him if you had a business sales rep out selling for you, would you hire someone like John who is assertive and consistent and keeps calling, or would you hire the person who when told you're not interested, you would never hear from again. Which one would you hire? He agreed: he would hire the assertive one.

So my call into the office that I was worried about ended up being a "That A Boy" and pat on the back at how happy he was to get the only calls like that about me. That day sticks to me like glue. I do not consider myself an aggressive person at all, but I had been through a pretty rough time prior to this. I needed the work, I had a family, and I was intimidated by all the other polished reps. I really set myself apart as a distinguished cold caller. Selling postage meters, folding machines, weighing devices, and mailroom equipment was a high-end leased sale; in most cases they were very expensive devices.

I was later given a mentor who took me under his wing and helped me sell one of the largest deals in the district. It was very complicated and technical, and I would have never been able to complete the sale without him. But it was one of those deals that put me into First Honors. I did my share of work. It wasn't just handed to me. I was involved all the way from start to finish, and it happened to be with a local Peoria University with a previous business contact that I had made while at Motorola. Here is a real business match making experience that I arranged using my meeting skills and my previous contact and knowledge of being able to match a customer with a business and a product; this helped seal the deal based on trust. The client later told me that our previous relationship was a big part of why she made the decision to go with us and secure the deal.

So I played a big influence on that one. This has showed me the power of whom you know and how building relationships and trust in business is a very important part of becoming successful.

Unfortunately, I did not stay at Pitney Bowes very long. But my story here is showing my desire to take things to a new level and using the skills I knew I had to make connections and that nothing happened until the meeting was set. This is consistent in what I have done up to this point and getting bored quickly with the norm. Looking back, and keeping with the theme of this book, once again, I was selling meetings. Yes it was my responsibility to sell and produce, but I was better at creating the first step in the process.

The demise of my career at Pitney Bowes was due to a new manager I clashed with and a big difference in our personalities. I gave my notice and left. My District Director tried real hard to keep me on board, but I was no longer interested in being managed the way the new guy was trying. Now, I am thinking, what am I going to do? As with all areas of my career, I say what does any of this have to do with selling or setting meetings? It shows a trend—a trend on my actions to seek something better and more satisfying, and to make my own path with what I do best. I don't know it's all leading me to do something greater than myself.

13 SEARCHING FOR MY CRAFT

Well here I am now in the spring of 1999 and unemployed. I did not have something lined up yet because the departure at Pitney Bowes was abrupt and unplanned. So starting another business was still not on the radar, and having a family was more important than anything else. Besides, I didn't have anything I wanted to invent at the time or a business idea to launch. I feel everything is about timing, learning, and opportunities presenting themselves.

"The right thing at the wrong time is the wrong thing." - *Joshua Harris.*

I believe you do have to go out and create your own opportunities, so I did. I filled my time with a few odd jobs, one of which was back into Motorola distribution and this time I was hired as Regional Sales Manager at Segno Communications and was stationed in Bloomington Normal. It was cool to be back selling and designing communications systems. But in 2001, I received a call out of the blue from a Sprint PCS manager, when Sprint was on its way to becoming the next big cellular service. I wanted in.

After quickly interviewing with the Hiring Manager, I got the job. He was a great manager, and I could tell right away that we would get along, and he would let me do things my way, but in line with the team goals and as a team player. I think you can be both. I am a self-driven person, but I understand the importance of teams. If I am successful, then my boss will be successful, and the team will be successful.

He was clear that he would get me trained and set my targets, then let me go into the wild. He did exactly that and it was right up my alley. I could be part of an innovative product and service, but do it on my own and make it mine. Sprint PCS, which is now Sprint, hit the central Illinois area early in 2001. I loved it. It was the first era of digital PCS service, and it was unheard of to have long distance, voice mail, texting, and now, for the first time, no roaming fees included in your plan and, of all things, internet capability.

Internet access on a cellular phone was unheard of at this point. Add to that, there was even a camera feature. I felt revived and felt like this was just the opportunity I was looking for and could make it my own without forking out any cash to start a business.

What do I mean by making it my own? Well, because I could specialize in a given area of Sprint and become the expert—like being the expert at offering and setting up mobile email. This makes me an internal KPI or specialist in a niche, which they called a product specialist.

At this time, my mind was on overload again, thinking of how I could be the very best and take it to a new level. I was hired as a business sales representative and this would be the start of a long career change and new opportunities. I made as many cold calls as I could, and arranged meetings with just about every business in Central Illinois that would meet with me so that I could present the new services.

I even set up meetings within a meeting by setting up a table on a scheduled day to also sell to all the employees. Although it was fun, it was also exhausting. I had meeting after meeting after meeting, and I know the job would have been a lot less stressful if I had someone to support me in the sales process like I do today.

I mean, how cool would it be if all I had to do was set it up, but that's not how it works. Every meeting I attended was arranged, set, and sold by me; but if I had someone else to arrange them or do the closing, I would have accomplished even more.

Cold calling and canvassing is looked at as not being as difficult as the closing the sale. The people who do both and are good at it are called hunters. There are cold callers, hunters, and closers, and that's a lot for one person in my opinion.

Some sales organizations use telemarketing centers to arrange calls. For example, a lawn fertilizer company may have a telemarketer or scheduler call you and set the date for service, then the representative just shows up the day of the meeting and sprays your yard. He or she is also a service person. I am breaking all of this down at this point because I know we went through a lot of representatives at Sprint in my time, and those who could do it all like me stayed, weathered the storm, and crunched the quotas. But I met a lot of people who just weren't the right people for the job, didn't have the drive, or just didn't try hard enough.

I remember everyone fighting for the leads, as it got tougher and tougher to generate business. So you had to be good at generating your own leads and meetings, and that is why I survived. My point with all of this is to show how important finding the first meeting is. I made it through the rush of calls just coming in like a lot of other reps did, but when the call slowed down and it was time to generate leads and meetings, it all changed. Again, nothing happens until a meeting is set.

You must have the skills to generate leads and arrange the meetings. If you are a small business that has no sales representative or can't afford one you can always outsource to an organization like mine.

Sprint gave me experience as a business representative, and I had the opportunity to offer the latest in cellular technology, the likes of which no one had ever seen. I was inundated by sales opportunities and meetings by the hundreds, both from my own cultivating and from sheer volume of interest in the area. People wanted the service and I was in the right place at the right time, so I capitalized. But for entrepreneurs like myself, it's all about the rush of something new that excites us. We want more and can get bored very easily, then are already looking for the next best thing. Even if it's within a business or company we work for. There is an article about this I recently read and it's called "Why You Should Never Start Just One Business." It is written by Neil Patel, a contributor for *Entrepreneur.com*, and it states,

"Those who start lots of companies are guaranteed that life will never by boring."

Well you can do this while working for a business, as well, like I did with the sign company at Motorola.

14 BE HEALTHY OR LEARN THE HARD WAY

Although I had fun, and Sprint was a great learning experience, Sprint was probably one the most stressful jobs I have ever had in my life. I was around 37 years old at the time, and I was not really doing any exercise, traveling in different states, working long hours, and eating fast food. This is no joke: I remember late in the job having to go to the hospital due to my heart. It was a big scare. I thought I was invincible and would take customer calls at all hours; people would actually stop my car to talk about getting a good deal on a cell phone.

It was crazy but it taught me things about life and to stay healthy. It was my first real life changing experience. I was at one of my meetings that was actually at a hospital, of all places, and I remember feeling fine as the meeting started, but it soon turned bad quick.

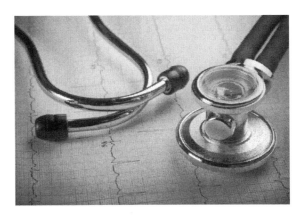

My heart started beating rapidly and I felt like I was going to pass out. I had no idea if it was a heart attack. The feeling of skipping beats was getting worse, and here I was sitting in front of a client at a hospital. Thank god it was towards the end of the meeting because somehow I remember making it through the meeting and acting like nothing was wrong, and I have no idea how the person couldn't tell I was having an issue.

I ended the meeting and left the hospital and drove across the street by myself to another hospital because that is where my insurance would be accepted. How crazy was that? I checked myself into the emergency room and was taken straight into my own room where they immediately connected me to an EKG machine to check my heart and started taking blood samples, etc. I was kept overnight and had to do a stress test and meet with the cardiologist. He explained the problem. They called it SVT, or Super Ventricular Tachycardia, which is a short in the electrical system. The doctor told me to stop drinking caffeinated products like coke and coffee, to stop eating bad food, and to go get healthy.

To make a long story short I am okay now, I just have to take medicine for the rest of my life. How fun is that? The point here is that it doesn't matter how successful you are, you have to take time for yourself and be healthy because money isn't everything.

15 STARTUP VENTURE OPPORTUNITY

As my Sprint experience becomes more involved, my drive to want to do more and to be innovative and specialize in a niche becomes more obvious. Sometime between 2001 and the end of my Sprint career in 2007, after hundreds of sales meetings, they rolled out a program called SBDN. SBDN is short for "Small Business Dealer Network," and it was designed to add business-to-business distributors to the marketplace through an indirect channel.

I was watching them role this out, and since I was successful at business-to-business selling, I wanted to be a part of it. I told my boss I wanted to transfer over, but not as a SBDN Manager, which I would later become, but as a SBDN dealer. It was a surprise, but here I go again wanting more, unsatisfied with what I had, and looking outside of the box, wanting to start another business.

This is a distributorship you have to apply for, not like an application for employment, but an application to be a franchise, so to speak. You have to have business experience, a business plan, financial wherewithal, support personnel, and an office.

So I had to document all this, then apply, and I'll be honest, my application was declined by Sprint Corporate due to my financials. We all know that a business plan has to be in place and financials have to be in order to start any business, so this was my first experience in seeking funding or to try and find an investor.

Back then there was no such thing as crowdfunding, only bank financing, personal lines of credit, and angel investors. All of this was critical for me to do what I do today. I was being schooled in the art of entrepreneurship before it was popular, and I remember writing a business plan tailored to speak to an investor. I remember hearing about a group of local angel investors that would look at deals in Peoria, and I had also heard of Score, which is a group of retired businessmen offering free advice and mentorship. I took advantage of all of these things, and I ended up setting a meeting to present my plan to the group of investors in Peoria. I remember feeling good about it and getting feedback. However, I did not secure any funding so I turned to an individual investor I had met back while I was with the Motorola Dealership. His name was Mike.

Mike was someone I met while trying to install an outdoor LED moving message sign on a building he owned in a high traffic area in Galesburg, IL. We had discussed a possible deal and it never went through, but I made a contact and made an impression on a key player in the community who had a reputation for investing in new opportunities. This part of my journey is important because it illustrates my ability to think and react quickly, and to jump on opportunities when I see them.

You hear about the Shark Tank investors telling you to never give up and be resourceful. I think this is a key trait that I did not know I had, and I did not hesitate to make these calls and set up the meetings when I was in the middle of a great idea.

So I called Mike up, told him a brief description of my idea, and set an appointment. Obviously, I said enough to capture his interest. The meeting went well and to my surprise, I had my first investor and was able to secure the funding and resubmit the Sprint SBDN application. We were approved to be an Indirect Sprint Business Dealer.

It was an exhilarating feeling, and I felt like I was ten feet tall. I was an official Sprint distributor and the business was called "Wireless Planet Express." Now I have to get an office, order inventory, execute a marketing plan, and get started. Oh boy, was this a highlight in my life. I really was on cloud nine, because I was already on fire with great sales and now I was able to convert them to my own business and did. I remember coming up with some very creative ideas; so much so that I caught the attention of Sprint corporate again, which I will tell you more about in a bit.

16 APPLYING STRATEGIES

My first plan was to go on site to the local colleges where students and parents would go to get registered for college. This was usually near a bookstore where I would set up a Sprint tent out front to sell and activate phones. Let me tell you, it was a lot—hundreds in fact. I sold so many phones and, if I can be honest, made a ton of cash. I took my entrepreneurial spirit and made it my own.

I continued the success and was the first to set up shop, kiosk style, inside Hy-Vee grocery stores. I would work a deal with the store manager, then set up on weekend's right in the front entrance where people were walking in, making us the first things they saw. I feel this was the start of the new store-in-a-store concept, and I was on the leading edge, but with a tent.

I would get customers applications for service, tell them to go shop, and when they came back out, I would have the phone ready. I mean, no one was going to the store to buy a phone; they were going there to buy groceries. But we would be their first stop. It was great. I even took my kids with me a few times, and they loved it.

I had such a great relationship with Hy-Vee that I was already on to another new idea. I set up my own display rack of wireless accessories and had my own space on the grocery sales floor, where I had an unmanned display rack POP (point of purchase) display, and the stores would sell my product for me. It was my first real experience with selling product in a store.

Life was good. So good, in fact, that Sprint contacted me and asked if I would be interested in opening up a Sprint Branded retail store. I wasn't really a retail kind of guy, but I wanted to expand, and that is where they wanted me to go. They would support it as a partner so I went.

Now on my third venture at Sprint, I opened up the first wireless kiosk in the Galesburg mall and then in a brand new outdoor shopping center in Peoria. I was growing, adding employees, and gaining market share, and Sprint loved me. I was a premier dealer.

Looking back, this all lends to my ability to be creative and build a brand. It taught me how to stand out from the crowd and showed me that I can get things done. I have to admit I also enjoyed the feeling of accomplishment and the satisfaction of knowing that it was my idea. Even though it was Sprint's brand, I was branding my company and myself. After signing up as a retailer I hit the market hard. This is where I personally learned the power of marketing and again, my mind is on overload.

17 LEARNING MARKETING

So now what? I took the most popular medium available for mobile phones, which in my professional opinion, was billboards. There were no social media sites yet, and the only thing I can remember is MySpace, which seemed to be for individuals, and I certainly did not recognize the value of it yet.

At the time, People were starting to become mobile; hence, I started targeting the Galesburg area with mobile phones. For one, it wasn't too expensive and, two, the space was available. I once heard that a local attorney was so popular because he signed an exclusive deal with a billboard company and almost owned all the good spots. It turned him into a superstar. I didn't know that then, I was acting on my own marketing knowledge and saw the opportunity; in my own words, I owned Galesburg, IL.

It was my market for the taking, and I took it. I had billboards on all the major streets and locations, and it was great. I later opened two new inline store locations, one in the Galesburg Mall, graduating from a kiosk to a store, and second, a new inline retail store in Peoria in a high-traffic strip mall. I still kept the kiosk in place, so I now have two locations in Peoria and was up to around 13 employees, counting my wife, who also worked for the company, and myself. It truly was great. I had money in the bank and enough to expand and add staff as needed.

During the later part of this journey, somewhere prior to the last year, which was 2007, I was approached by another dealer and by competitive wireless giant Nextel. I added Nextel to my product lineup and started selling in new markets especially B2B. I am now learning how to operate a business compared to my earlier sign business. I did well and later sold it to an employee.

18 MANAGEMENT EXPERIENCE

The upper management at Sprint seemed to like me, and I was known for connecting people to products. So now another new opportunity is coming my way as Regional Manager of Indirect Channel, which includes managing a very large territory from southern Illinois to clear up in the northern part of Michigan, like Muskegon.

The salary offer was great, and it was time for me to look for the next best thing and try something new. This is consistent so far in my career: I always want more or something new and like to have several opportunities in my options bucket. You always hear when you're hot your hot and when you're not you're not. So I took the position and managed the Illinois Sprint dealer network for over a year and the experience would later translate into another role we will talk about in the book.

Although this sounded exciting, it's not really who I am. I know this today that: I am not a manager. I didn't know this at the time, but I do not consider myself a very good for it. I did not know I would be out of my element, but I gave it a shot and, like I said, it lasted about a year. Like the quote says, "I never fail, as long as I am learning I am succeeding".

I did what I could, but I am not a manager of other people; I am a sales guy. Now, I have to manage the training and sales for wireless at Best Buy, Walmart, Radio Shack, and the entire indirect dealer channel, like the one I just came from with my own stores. I had staff and upper management to report to and it was grueling.

I remember reading hundreds of emails. It seemed to be the same with conference calls, stuck in an office a lot and not out making deals. I had employees to do that, and I had to manage. When they weren't doing well, I had to try and figure out how to help them. I was the type of manager that could take you with me and show you how I would do the job, but not the type of manager who encouraged and lifted you up. I was too friendly and not a manager; the staff members were my friends.

Of course, management is no longer what people want, its leadership they need, so you would think that would have been a good fit for me, but it wasn't.

Remember the Daymond John quote earlier, which says entrepreneurs will succeed, succeed, fail then succeed. This is exactly what is happening to me. I thought management leadership meant, let me show you how it's done. Maybe it was, and I do believe that is what is needed today, but it was still a challenge to motivate, and that's where I started to lose traction with staff. Then I also started to lose interest because that is not my creative side. I was not becoming my manager's boss's favorite person.

My immediate manager believed in me, but his boss was losing faith. Somehow right around when all this was taking place, an outside dealer called me and wanted to hire me to manage his business-to-business operations and help open new stores. Chuck is his name, and he is a doctor who just happened to own a Nextel Store and somehow heard about my B2B sales experience and contacted me.

19 RESEARCHING MYSELF AND MY SKILLS

This is where I believe I am starting to get the feeling people are noticing me for my skills, and I believe I am now learning to become a KPI in sales calls. The new dealer opportunity was someone just like me, only he operates in Macomb, IL, and he had aspirations of adding a new location in Galesburg, which is right up my alley. I know how to open and launch a new store, hire staff, make signs, market, find management, and then do B2B sales myself. This is the area I shine in, so I took the offer and made the move.

Now this new position still allows me to represent Sprint, so it wasn't like I left Sprint high and dry. Plus I was still able to negotiate taking some named business accounts with me. Life was good again. I was back in my element and on my own, and not being held down by all of the red tape, conference calls, training people, responding to emails, etc. I loved it, and we did launch the new Galesburg store with the Sprint and Nextel combo, along with later adding the new prepaid market through Virgin Mobile.

I was again taking what I do best to the next level and trying to grow the business, and I do feel a sense of satisfaction when I can help others. Yes, I am making money, but it's even better if I've helped someone with their goal. I was reinventing or rediscovering myself, and I was realizing more and more my place in the work world and not to try and be something I am not.

I feel it is okay to look at all opportunities in life, but to also know your core competencies and niche. This doesn't happen overnight, and I do not believe you know this right away. It takes time and experience to find it, and I was doing just that. I tried something new and gave it a shot, but got out while I could and before I became stressed out again.

The big management positions are now on my resume and LinkedIn profile, and I am proud of the opportunities I had. I owe a big thanks to two Sprint hiring managers who I really enjoyed working with. Like all other names I mention in this book, I will keep it to first names only, Joe and Tony. They both became good friends, and I definitely looked up to them as mentors. Tony was my first manager at Sprint when I first started, and he is still to this day a good friend. He has actually called me several times over the years offering me new opportunities for work. Joe and I stay in touch every now and then.

20 SOCIAL MEDIA NETWORKS

Speaking of LinkedIn, I would like to talk about this real quick, before moving on to my next venture. If you are not using LinkedIn today, you should because by the time this is published it will have already been available to business professionals for many years. Having become real popular in 2006, as of 2015, it now has more than 400 million business professionals using it. It's a tool I use today for making connections, and I tie into my cold calling and research.

What I really wanted to say is that somewhere along the line a mentor told me to capture all of your successes in a book, and that is kind of like LinkedIn, but more like a bragging book not like a publication or a novel but in a bound book you make yourself. I call it "Lifetime Achievements." I had this well before LinkedIn was available, but I had no way to share it with all my business connections.

So what is different from a resume or a profile on LinkedIn versus this? Well, this is where you assemble on paper copies of achievements, contracts you secured, awards, business deals, maybe large commission checks, business cards, degrees, certifications, and anything else you have achieved in your lifetime inside or outside of work. I have mine and it needs to be updated, but if I am ever in another interview, I would take it with me, and it makes a great leave behind and brag book, and I believe separates yourself from all the other applicants and when you're gone for family, colleagues, and friends.

I recommend a professional to help you with your LinkedIn profile and to have a paid makeover done if you haven't. I also use Twitter, Facebook, YouTube, and some Instagram, but not all of these are for my personal profile. Most are for my businesses today. But you will want to utilize social media if you want to market, brand, and raise your profile. We will talk more about this in the later chapters.

21 STILL SEARCHING FOR MY PERFECT CRAFT

As I was about to end my career with Sprint in early 2007, I received a call from a job recruiter regarding a business development position at Insert Frontier Communications. I knew I was going to be leaving so I did take the offer, and was not employed there very long. In fact, I was only there about a year. I am mentioning it because it is part of everything I have done, and it is another one of the jobs that you never know if you will like or not. If nothing else, I did have telecom experience and enjoyed that.

However this is the landline side of the telecom world, and I was in the wireless world. I did meet a couple of really great salespeople and managers and have them as professional connections on LinkedIn, and I feel if I ever had to reach out to them I could.

Although this was not for me, I did enjoy one aspect of the short time there and I remember traveling to Carlinville, Illinois for long periods of time, and it was to launch a wireless network for the city of Carlinville operated by

Frontier Communications. I made the cover of the Frontier Communications marketing tabloid for being part of that launch, so this was another taste of star quality.

Here I was on the front cover and had the bragging rights to anyone at Frontier. I stated that it wasn't for me, but remember this was a wireless network installation and I really enjoyed it. We had to cold call and contact all the local businesses, restaurants, and coffee shops to see if they wanted to offer the service as Wi-Fi connectivity in their establishments.

I was focused and trying my best to make the other part of my job a success, but I did not like the landline side as much as I thought I would. It may not have been the equipment sales part of it I didn't enjoy, it may have been that I was servicing a rural market and all my previous experience was in large markets.

So I quickly started to think about an idea I already had been considering, and before I left it was already in the works. I did somewhere in the neighborhood of 20 new sales calls per week trying to get business lined up, and for the short time I was there I did well with the numbers. But I just wasn't happy. I wanted more than just working for someone else.

22 BUYING AND SELLING BUSINESSES

So, before talking about my next professional career allow me to set the stage for this one, because I am about to take a very interesting turn unlike anything I have done so far.

Way back before I really even left the Sprint world, I was starting to think back about my days there and how I was helping dealers expand, grow and look for new locations. So when you think about my job, I was acting as a liaison or a broker. I would help the owners start a store from scratch, working with business plans, financials, scouting locations, etc.

This started me thinking that I would like to be a broker for a living and start a career at connecting business, people, and products. So sometime late in 2006, I had written a thread on a website called GoBigNetwork. This site was used to look for investors and share your business ideas on what you want to do. It was before startup groups like 1 Million Cups and StartUp Grind, where you could present your ideas for consideration. I thought it was pretty cool, so I joined and posted a thread stating that I had great experience as a Sprint Store owner and helping others grow and find new locations or merging into larger ones by way of acquisition.

So I asked on the thread if anyone was interested in my knowledge and stated that I thought this was an untapped market and concept. A company out of New York called Bridge Business and Property replied. It was the founding owner who said he would love to hear more and would like to talk about me joining his team of business brokers as a Managing Partner.

I will be honest, I couldn't believe it. So we went through all the application and interviewing processes, conversations, and phone calls, and he made me an offer. It was my first venture back out on my own because this was a commission position, so I had to be certain it would work. It sounded great, and I soon had to take Illinois Real Estate Courses and get a certificate to do business as a broker in the state of Illinois. By time this was all ready, it was December 2006.

By January 2007, I was ready to go and was going to use my wireless startup knowledge and industry contacts to focus on helping wireless retailers of all brands buy out other locations or sell theirs. So basically I am selling meetings that connect people. I remember ordering business cards, car door magnets for advertising, folders, and brochures from Bridge Brokers corporate, because I already had parties interested in selling their business.

It is a long sales cycle, and it is a very confidential type of business. There is a lot of paperwork with letters of intent, non-disclosures, valuating the business, getting tax information, and seller's information, including sales, debt info, assets, and so much more. We take all this information and create a website listing just like is done for a real estate deal. They are listed on the Bridge Brokers site but a lot of larger national sites like Business for Sales.com. Sometimes you are representing both sides of the deal, and that is really tricky. But I knew a lot about running a wireless store, so I knew what to look for. I started a relationship with the wireless franchise giant Wireless Toyz, but at the same time I knew I would have to diversify and so I started another relationship with Quiznos.

So where did Quiznos come from out of the blue, when I had a wireless communications background? I think it was because I had a buyer looking for restaurant equipment contact me, and I found another guy who would later even become a boss who was closing a restaurant. So I matched them up and let them work out a deal, and I just facilitated it all.

That led me into the restaurant side. So it seems this part of my story is jumping around, and it is because it is easy to do. I had so much going on, and it was new and exciting. There were several big ventures I gained from being in this business from late 2006 to early 2010. The biggest thing is to do your homework and work hard and not be tempted by the fact your self-employed.

Because no one is looking over your shoulder and asking questions, you must get up every day and make the calls and set the meetings. You're defined by what you do when others are not looking. I had wireless customers coming at me left and right, wanting help. My largest account was a local wireless dealer.

So here is the deal of the century, or at least for this particular venture in my life. I caught word through a friend that this local wireless dealer wanted to sell and get out, so I did what I've learned to do best: do an initial visit, followed up with calls, and eventually set up an meeting asking for a few minutes of their time to introduce myself and my company, and learn a little bit more about them, as well, so the opportunity is mutual. If all else fails, I will have made a new business connection.

23 BE CAREFUL WHAT YOU ASK FOR

My efforts finally paid off, and I was in the office of the seller. I was calm, collected, and confident. After a brief presentation of what I could offer, I learned more about what they needed, and before I knew it the natural flow led me right to a signed contract. A contract to sell the wireless dealer stores and I knew I could. I had the contacts, and everyone I knew wanted to expand.

The asking price was over one million dollars, and I remember not reacting to it. My sales training kicked in, but inside I was thinking, "Wow, I hit the jackpot and another milestone in my professional career." Remember, this was just the contract signing to sell the business and collect the financial history to go along with it. I remember getting it all filled out and putting the agreement in my file folder, but never looked at it to see if the client signed. I mean why would I look to see, because they agreed, shook hands, and filled it out, even printing their names and title.

So I thought it was there, and I went on to start the process of listing the stores for sale, getting store pictures, financial data, and getting the listing approved. Everything we did together was on a mutual basis and agreement along the way. I tell you this story because it is one of the most valuable lessons of my career, and it effected my decision to continue on as a broker.

I never even thought about it the whole time I am setting up buyer meetings for this business. Again, they were complying with everything I asked for. To give you ideas of the potential here, remember I said it was over a million-dollar sale and my contract stated the commission would be 10%. I was looking at a $100,000 commission. Is that motivating? Well, of course it is. That kind of money would have kept me in operation for several more years, if I used it correctly.

So I worked hard to find larger dealers to buy them because that would make the most sense. I even talked with a corporate wireless carrier about the possible transfer, and they were okay with it. The buyer signed all the necessary paperwork and gave letters of intent and bank letters showing they could fund it. Everything was perfect.

We did have to go back and forth a few times, and then one

day, while I was doing my due diligence with another follow-up, I found out that the owner, the person who signed my exclusive agreement, had decided to go into negotiations with internal staff for them to do an employee purchase.

But in either case I would have still been eligible for my commission based on the exclusive agreement. Unfortunately, the owner stopped communicating with me, and I became frustrated and looked to my corporate legal department for support and direction and we ended up hiring a local business contract attorney to work this case as a breach of contact. This process was long, tedious and took years, well after I left doing the business brokering.

I had to send everything I had including my own statements of the meetings, emails, paperwork, conversations, meetings, etc. The defendant stated he was never able to even do the sale because he did not have the board's approval.

Honestly, it was very surprising knowing that we were acting in full agreement on making a sale happen. I was never told anytime during the process that they would not sell. I mean, I did everything, and I knew I could get the job done and have offers well past the million-dollar mark.

So after years of court depositions, meetings, and court appearances, we finally received an offer to settle out of court for a tenth of the amount it was supposed to be. So how depressing was that? I was glad it was over and that we were recognized as being in the right, but being completely exhausted by it and the legal system, we agreed to take the offer and be done.

It is a lesson to me I would later use during my inventing stage of use of agreement signatures. You always hear people tell you to get paperwork signed when you are dealing with business, even when it comes to friends and family, and I now have told many people my experience and that I have learned to document everything. So does any of this have anything to do with selling or connecting people? Yes, it does. It prepared me for paying attention to the details, being ready with all the documents, and having everything you need with you.

Later on in the book, when I discuss my invention, you will hear me tell an interesting story about getting paperwork signed and business friends thinking it is humorous. What I also find interesting is that I hold no hard feelings on the deal and view it as a learning experience.

To sum up what we have learned about me so far: I know I have the drive to just go out on my own and open a new business as an entrepreneur; I know I have a bit of an inventors mindset because I designed a new advertising sign that wasn't available yet; I've had some valuable business lessons; I know that I am not shy about asking for funding; I've learned how to sell meetings effectively I've seen the insides and outside of other businesses and what makes them successful and not successful; I've been mentored by many great people; and I am great at connecting people, business, and products. I also know what I am not so good at. This is all ramping me up for what is about to come. I still do not label myself as an entrepreneur, writer, or even an inventor yet. So let's continue, and hopefully I have caught your attention by now because we are almost halfway through.

24 A NEW BEGINNING

It is somewhere near December 2008 and this story will take us to around June of 2010. In 2008 I was reacquainted with a restaurant owner—the one I mentioned earlier, whom I said I would come back to later in the book. His name is Fred, and originally when I met him, he had already been in the restaurant business and was leaving. We made a good business connection and I found out he was hiring and was already running another successful website design company. I was already very interested in promoting businesses and offering online marketing, but building websites for a living also really interested me.

This was not something I really had thought about, and it certainly was not planned. At this stage I am just going through what life is putting in front of me. The only website experience I have had up to this point was hiring a company to build me one while I was running my wireless stores at Sprint.

Well, I am leaving out a part of my life that was so brief I wasn't even going to mention it. But now I realize I should. That is, I took a job for a phonebook company for less than a year. I did not like selling advertising for phonebooks, but I did like their new presence in website design and online marketing, aka, the beginning of social selling. And a phonebook company was starting to revolutionize what they offer and started a section within their business model to sell online ads to go with print; but we also started selling small websites and offering search engine optimization.

Now this was brand new and I loved it. In fact, I was the top sales person and was real good at connecting people to the right online solution for a short time before leaving. Why? Because it was new and exciting, and "new and exciting," I am learning, is what keeps me motivated. I have recently read an article that was in *Entreprenuer.com* and it was titled "Why You Should Never Start Just one Business."

It explains that those who start lots of businesses are serial entrepreneurs and if you have started one company, you can do it again. And you probably should. Starting Multiple Businesses guarantees that life will never be boring. Entrepreneurship is a rush, and although I wasn't starting another business of my own, I was searching for something new. Just like starting a new business, I was starting fresh again and could always find my own way.

25 BACK TO THE BASICS

When I went to work for Fred at Online Innovative Creations, I was hired as their business development guy until around June of 2010. I had a great experience and met some more good friends who have later supported my new idea in inventing. But wait there is more. Yes, that statement from AsSeenonTV again. I cannot help it, it seems to be stuck in my mind now... as I laugh and write. Fred was a pretty laid back guy and I liked that. He was also inspiring to me at the time because here was another successful business entrepreneur I am getting acquainted with, and so he was cool with letting me decide how I wanted to operate. I believe he recognized the fact that I know business development and can generate my own leads and meetings. I still had reports to do and results to show, but I was able to apply the same energy I received at the phonebook company doing website design sales to Fred's business.

So I started marketing, making dozens and hundreds of sales calls, setting meetings, following up, and closing some deals. I filled my funnel of prospects and started to create my system again, and I remember having the feeling around the office that I was thought of as somewhat of a sales pro. I even had the feeling from the web developers there that I was a sales rock star. Or maybe they were just very good at knowing what motivated me?

I knew this was the first real sales person that they hired so I have to deliver, and I know the numbers game. I know activity eventually results in new business opportunities. I have it in my head how this will all take place. All my continuous efforts on making sales calls, onsite prospect visits, the email and phone follow-up, and setting meetings all fell into place just like I knew it would. I started using a database to collect it all with and soon had a repetitive sales system that would cultivate meetings, guaranteed.

It was very refreshing and I had no idea I could teach others or would ever document this cold calling system later in life. I did this successfully for about a year and a turning point came to me again, just like it always has. Sometimes it comes to me sooner than later and in this case it was sooner. I remembered seeing a guy that kept coming into Fred's office and having meetings about sales for OICG, and I thought I was the only person selling direct for Fred.

Of course in business, you create networks, connections, and even your staff is always selling. But this guy would be in and out and the meetings where always brief. One day I asked who he was and who he worked for, and he tells me he is an independent rep for this business alliance that I am part of. It is a group of other local businesses that come together and formed an alliance and offer different services that are complimentary of each other, which allows them to be a complete source for technology needs, permitting each one to operate in their core competency.

I thought that idea was pretty cool, but I didn't do anything about it because he already had the job and I had mine.

Besides, I was kind of getting tired of trying to find my niche and had been through several short job cycles recently. But as I said shortly after being on board, I had heard that the alliance guy I had been seeing was leaving and had to move away, and I thought to myself: I want his job.

I eventually approached Fred and explained it's not like I would be leaving him and web design, because doesn't this job support you directly and several others, and it does. It happened that I received a unanimous vote from the alliance owners and I transferred over.

So here I am again in a very short period of time job hoping, already moving on, and starting another entrepreneurial role. This may also be attention deficit disorder? If so, I had a bad case of it. I honestly did not know it was just a period of time where nothing seemed to fit. I was dying to do something I felt comfortable with, and this was a new opportunity that I could make it my own.

26 BUSINESS DEVELOPMENT

From March 2009 to the present, I am an independent contractor for Prairie Technology Alliance. I am a self-employed entrepreneur fulltime and I call my business *business453*. This will be the longest part of my story. I will finally lead you to how I became an inventor of, not only a product, but of a way of capturing my craft in sales and eventually writing my story, "Nothing Happens Until The Meeting is Set" connecting people, business, and products.

Let's talk about my time at Prairie Technology Alliance, and why I was initially so attracted to it and why I am still here. As an entrepreneur, this would be a good fit for me because it's new, just getting started, and I am a Startup contractor on the ground floor of a great opportunity.

The first thing I noticed was the advertising they were and some of the accounts the previous rep was developing. Man, I was excited. I will be honest, the commissions was not the greatest—but what startup ever is—but it still attracted me, and I now have five companies I can represent, and how exciting and challenging would that be.

It's new, fresh, and I can develop it, be on my own again, create new n business connections, get my own insurance, and support myself as an independent business. I have instantly inherited five customers in the technology field, five wanting me to do business development, generate leads, and confirm qualified meetings for them.

I love challenges, especially if it's with a startup, so I hit the ground running, trying to learn as much as a could about each one and develop an action plan. It was tough at first, only because of the money, and like any startup it takes time to develop and business sales funnel. I did it, though. I hit the road, planned my calls, and targeted clients. I remember the first two years just making it by, knowing that at least I still had a great variety of products and services and could always switch it up if the tough got going.

My mission was to build client relationships and find new business opportunities for the group. I counted the number of sales calls I had to make, I was good at building new business and became pretty well known for prospecting in the central Illinois area. I would target 20 companies a week, and although that may not sound like a lot, let me assure you, that week after week, month after month, it adds up because you are carrying over prospects from the week prior every single time. I call it a multiplier.

I would get names from the local Chamber of Commerce; off trucks, cars, and buildings that I would pass in traffic; as well as from networking events and from the contacts of the businesses they would ask me to target.

Once I would have the list, I would do my research online via the internet, and then I would have a name as to who to call on. Earlier, I mentioned you would get every single detail about my prospecting efforts and formula, but I will save that for the end. For now, I wanted to just give you an idea of all the calls I have made. You figure 20 a week times seven years and that comes to 7,280 suspects that week after week would multiply out because I have to do follow-up. Some become meetings, while others I have to keep calling over and over again. It becomes repetitive, and that's how I was able to get so good at it.

I later brought on a sixth business to the alliance that ended up joining them. For several in the alliance, it's a great deal because as a smaller business it is a way to get a fulltime rep for a sixth of the cost. The concept was conceived by Brian and his partner Fred; they started Prairie Technology Alliance.

These two operate a website development company and information technology, computers and service side and they also have a security systems, telecom and ink company as part of the alliance. These guys are all local business owners and entrepreneurs and the sixth one I added early on is a confidential paper and hard drive destruction company.

After several years of ramping up my activities, I started making more money, and the time and effort I was putting in was starting to pay off. I was getting to the point where I could predict the number of leads or appointments I would get just based on my activities, including the number of visits and follow-up calls I would make—it was all systematic. Soon I was officially and finally a successful business on my own, well, as an independent contractor anyway.

My time at Prairie Tech was more than just prospecting for sales; I was, and still am, responsible for confirming the meetings and arranging member introductions for a specific client's need or an assessment.

After several years, I started attending more and more business functions like Chamber of Commerce networking events, speed networking, breakfasts, luncheons, dinners, and even local tradeshows. If you add all of this into the sales prospecting mix, plus what I was already doing, it multiplied my efforts and all the face-to-face networking became easier to produce a lead.

I set up the meeting, made the introductions, and steered the meetings toward the member company, and when it was all done I still had follow-up to do. In the last couple of years I started working on social media accounts, like Facebook, and especially now on LinkedIn, as another means of cultivating contacts and leads.

You still have to go through a similar process, but it's a softer approach and less intrusive as walking in a place of business. It's called social selling, and it is the most popular form of getting acquainted because now it acts as a two-way communication. You can post relevant content, say happy birthday or happy work anniversary, comment on their posts to get engaged in a conversation, or ask a mutual acquaintance to introduce you.

This saves a walk-in cold call now. However, if I'm having difficulties getting a return reply, I will still revert to an unannounced cold call walk-in. I will give more details on this area later in the book. As an independent contractor for Prairie Technology Alliance, I am my own business, and like I said earlier, it's called *business453*. Later in the years I decided to bring it to the full public eye by creating a website and writing this book. I will talk more about that later. After meeting Kevin Harrington and reading his KPI book, I am realizing now that I have to go from the past to the future and back in time again for this story to unfold. They are all related, and until I started writing I never knew it would all tie together. The website is *www.business453.com* and it should be done when this book prints.

About half way through my seven years as business453, I was asked to speak at a local conference called the *Women in Leadership Conference*. The host of the conference wanted someone to speak to about lead generation, because every business wants to know how to create leads for themselves. This is especially true for small startups where most are the owner, the sales person, and the bookkeeper—they do it all and so how can they generate leads.

I just happened to be known for becoming the king of cold calls, and it was finally then I realized I should document my system called ***Effective & Proven Techniques for Acquiring New Sales Meetings!*** We will cover this in detail near the end of the book.

But even then I wasn't thinking anything about becoming any more than I already was as a business development professional, and I remember the audience at the conference, maybe 75 or so in attendance, giving me all their focus as I discussed and presented the stops for acquiring new sales leads. It is amazing how many small businesses are hungry for the knowledge, especially those who are the owner and have to do everything themselves. I will come back to this part in a little bit.

27 CREATING A NEW IDEA

In this chapter, I have to take a turn or shift away from business development and discuss the process of inventing and all the aspects of creating a product, and how I still apply business and sales skills when doing so. I will list each one out like a school curriculum because you learn each step and it is just like a workshop or a program with each one showing me something I may or may not have known. In this case it was learning how to truly bring a patented invention down a path to where I am today.

The end of this chapter will eventually tie back to where I am today and bringing me to my meeting the Shark, Kevin Harrington, and learning what I am really good at. In the process I hope you are able to pick up a few tips that I learned by doing.

After a few years at Prairie Technology Alliance, I met a girl from Cedar Rapids, Iowa, and for some reason that spirit I have for starting something new also drives my personal life as well. I decided I would ask the guys if I could move and keep my job and travel two or three days of the week back to my market in Peoria, IL. I could then spend the other days on follow-up, emails, and doing some marketing in the new area as well to see what I could cultivate.

Plus, several of the companies can do business anywhere, and it did not matter where our home office was. (This part will eventually make sense so please hang in there.) After a long debate they agreed; we would try it and see if this could work. It actually did. I was a very lucky person because they let me make the move, and I was thinking at some point I may have to switch jobs, but I am glad I didn't and I am glad the members I worked for saw value in me and my performance.

I remember getting up and not thinking twice about the two and half hour drive from Cedar Rapids, IA to Peoria, IL, traveling several days a week and living in a local Peoria hotel 128 times; this is the life of a road warrior. The hotel staff and management became my friends and eventually offered me holiday gifts. The check-in process became so easy and I would sometime just walk-in and the keys were on the front desk if the staff was available. Sometimes I would even get the same room and view, all because they knew me. It was great customer service and it was like a home away from home.

You are probably wondering what does this have to do with sales calls, right? It shows the lifestyle and my dedication to get the job done no matter what. Grant Cardone, the greatest salesman ever according to his marketing and social media, is always advertising to do whatever it takes to get the job done.

Here is where the inventing part of my life comes along, and now I am about to make my own product. My girlfriend at the time was a hairstylist, and her official title at the JC Penny Styling Salon was Master Stylist. She had been there for 13 years with a nice client base and seemed very happy and content. She would come home from time to time and show me finger cuts caused by her shears. It didn't seem to be a big deal to her, and they would put a band-aid on and she would go back to work. If it was real bad, they would also wrap it with what they called a finger condom, and that would keep it secure and prevent blood from getting on anyone.

Well one day I received a call that she had cut herself so bad that they sent her to the emergency room and they had to apply surgical glue on the wound. I remember thinking, "this is crazy," and asking, "how often does this happen?" She said she couldn't remember exactly but it was a lot.

So I went to the internet to see what I could find, and I would just buy her something to protect her fingers and knuckles. I knew there were PPE Gloves out there, as well as cut resistant gloves, but nothing designed for cosmetologists and hairstylists. Plus, after talking with her further about it they do not want to wear anything, nor have they ever been offered any protective wear.

Finger Cut Protection by CosmoGlove

I had already started watching *Shark Tank* on ABC, the hit show about entrepreneurs who invent products and have ideas who go on TV and pitch to investors and get their product out and into the market in a big way.

So I started thinking, I wonder if I could do this? I had no experience in this area, but boy do I have the drive. Everything I have been learning was how to do things on my own, and the school of life and business 101 were gearing me up, and I was just waiting for the right time and right opportunity. I asked her, "If you would wear anything to protect yourself from further injury what would it need to too look like?"

She informed me that the cuts are always on two fingers, the index and middle fingers and the knuckles, so just buy me something for that. I wanted to help her so I got on the internet just like anyone would do, and I searched for gloves and found hundreds, but none that are designed like she wanted.

I couldn't find anything. So guess what? This is where I got my second start in inventing. I still had no idea that this is what I would be doing. I honestly didn't. It was really just me trying to come up with something for her to wear.

I suppose this is that drive I have to keep evolving, to be creative, and to start something new. I ordered cut resistant gloves and started modifying them, and came up with four or five different styles, which she tried on. We even agreed that she should take them to the salon and get the others girls she worked there to offer opinions as well. So she did this, and a lot of time went by and the feedback came back that they agreed on a two-finger, half-palm glove, which is now available at http://www.cosmofingerguard.com.

The only problem then was that there was no such thing, and it did not exist on the market. The one mockup we had was a full five-finger, full-palm glove that I had to hack up and sew in an elastic liner so that it would stay tight across the palm. I didn't want to have to make them myself, so I started thinking that maybe I better find a glove manufacturer.

Here is where my cold calling business skills came in handy, because I called dozens of manufacturers and I wanted to have them sign a non-disclosure so they wouldn't steel my idea. The ones who wouldn't, I had to just explain you are not making it or what I want would already be available, and they would laugh and think I was crazy. How did I know if it wasn't already in their research and development? But I knew it wasn't because there was no one offering any type of glove for the beauty industry. They were all industrial, manufacturing, military, building trades, food, etc., but nothing for hairdressers.

But the ones who wanted to know more before shutting me down, I would need to get some protection and have them sign a non-disclosure before describing my glove or showing them drawings.

As I said, this all happened to be right around when the ABC hit show *Shark Tank* was starting to air. As it happened, that was my favorite reality show. I would be tuned in every Friday night and get really involved and that inspired me and taught me a few things. So the timing was great. I took what I already learned from business development and past business experience and what I was learning from the sharks and started to get all my documents in line. See, you never stop learning, even from TV.

I started creating my own non-disclosures, filed a provisional patent, and kept everything a big secret. I ordered a bunch of material from inventing companies thinking I would submit the idea to them. My cold calling skills where put to the test, and my persistence to create something new gave me drive. Imagine if you're a large glove manufacturer and you get a call from an unknown guy asking you to sign a non-disclosure, most would say "NO," and they did. I kept telling all of them I have a great idea for a safety glove, but I cannot tell you what it is.

I ended up talking to Dyneema and they are the company that invented this cut-resistant synthetic yarn I wanted to use even though most have not heard of it, though most are familiar with Kevlar. The research showed this was the latest cut-resistant technology and I wanted to be on the cutting edge if I am going to do this. No pun intended.

28 SELLING THE MANUFACTURE

I was getting no place fast with the manufacturers of gloves. I was just way too small and was unknown, and it was way too expensive to stop production for 100 gloves when they have orders for tens of thousands. So what am I going to do?

I've watched enough of Shark Tank to know that a lot of the inventors go to China and I didn't want to do that. Plus, I do not know anyone who I could trust. This is a major challenge but you have to be a critical thinker and make it happen and keep on going if I want to make this work.

So I decided to research the actual knitting machines that make cut-resistant gloves and found a company called Shima Seiki USA. They are the manufacturer of the computerized knitting machines that not only make gloves, they can also knit scarves, hats, sweaters, socks, and a bunch of other things... But they cost $125,000 dollars. I did not have that kind of money and even if I could raise it, I had no proof of my product other than a local group of stylists.

So I asked Shima if they could make the gloves for me. I

explained what I was doing and told them my vision and of course this was all after convincing them to sign a non-disclosure. I was able to convince them to sign it and they agreed to make me my first batch of specialty gloves. I set it all up—my selling skills and persistence all paid off. It shows you should never give up.

After all the rejections (and I am sure some even laughed at my requests), I was now about to get my first batch of prototypes for field-testing. But first I had to find who I could buy the cut-resistant yarn from, and that required more research, more phone meetings, and more persuasion. I went to the manufacture direct of the cut resistant yard for that and of course once again I am way to small and unknown, and not a licensed distributor of any product. But they finally gave me the name of a glove manufacturer in North Carolina who was a distributor of the yarns I needed, and they allowed me to buy enough raw materials to trial test, so I could make some glove samples. They also agreed to sign a non-disclosure, so now I am finally starting to feel like I getting some traction. I have glove materials and a company willing to make them, so off we go. To this day I think it's possible the manufacturer wanted to sell me a machine and that is probably why they agreed to make the first batch.

Here I am in business development still doing daily cold calls and arranging meetings for a technology firm in Peoria, IL now creating the world's first Cosmetology safety glove. I had Shark Tank to thank for that desire and ambition. So with all of this going on, Shark Tank would come on and I would get on Twitter and socialize with the Sharks and try to get traction that way. Sometimes they would interact, and I would say something about my idea thinking they would reply.

It's funny when you think about it because you have to get on the show for anything to happen, and people would tell me I should, but I knew it was way too early. I watched people come on the show with way more progress and a lot in sales and still get shot down, but it is still motivating me to finish developing the CosmoGlove.

I believe if it was not for my sales training, previous experience in trying to create a startup, desire to keep shooting for a "Yes", my previous mentors, and this TV show, I may have never did anything. It's true when they say it's all about timing, but it is also about recognizing the opportunity and seizing the moment and that my friend was instinct. I'm really not a person to pat himself on the back, but I recently read and wrote a great quote by Grant Cardone

"If you're not willing to promote yourself then why should anyone else? It's not shameful unless you're embarrassed about yourself or product."

29 LEARNING FROM A SHARK

I was watching Shark Tank one Friday evening and Daymond John announced he was going to partner up with an inventing company called Edison Nation. Someone would win the contest, which would include mentorship from Daymond, capital, and the ability to work with him and this inventing company.

The rules were pretty simple: just watch the show and pay attention to the details because the next day Daymond would Tweet a question about the show and you would have to put the answer on the Edison Nation website the next day. I was so tuned in it would seem funny to others.

I did this week after week and until the contest came to an end and even though I was not chosen I was one of his top ten fans, received an acknowledgement from him, and even received a signed copy of his latest book cover in Jet Set Magazine. That was so cool, and I was proud that I achieved the status even though I didn't win. I believe this drives me even more.

Nothing Happens Until The Meeting Is Set

The idea that I did not win made me even more determined. See I am so used to winning and getting the job done in sales and always getting the satisfaction of a confirmation, I wanted more. Behind the scenes we are getting our first sample of gloves in, our first website has been designed, our logo created, business cards, Facebook, the works. I am determined to make this happen and looking back it's all an amazing learning curve.

I filed for a provisional patent to get protection, and once I had that, I started to hit the road to visit local beauty salons and beauty schools. I remember putting my cold calling skills to the test and arranged visits and meetings and it was viewed as a hindrance.

However, I knew from the girls I was testing it with that it's a fact and that everyone will get cut, so for those who would shoot me down at the salon it was a pride thing. They were proud of their profession and wore the finger scars proudly as battle wounds. No one was really interested to be honest, and I made around 60 salon visits and meetings.

Some would just want me to leave a sample and we would. That's part of selling, especially with a new product never seen before. This is where I believe the average person would give up.

Remember the video earlier in this book I asked you to watch by Patrick Bet-David called *"The Life of an Entrepreneur in 90 Seconds"*? If you did not watch it, go ahead and take a quick break, Google it, watch it, and come back. It's perfect because he talks about all the rejections, the rumors, all the people telling him "NO." What would you do?

For me, all it did was challenge me and somehow I knew that the best ideas are the ones that others would criticize, and if they can't do it themselves then they will not want you to do it. Just like another earlier reference with Will Smith's movie. But it was more than that; I was a believer in the idea that hairdressers do have injuries with shears. No matter how good you are, accidents happen, some more severe than others and some requiring a visit to the emergency room. I saw it firsthand and witnessed it myself. It made me believe that if I didn't finish this someone else would.

I knew that I had come way too far, and I watched other ideas I felt had less of a problem solving impact as my CosmoGlove, and yet they are on TV and have sales. So if they can do it so can I. I've learned that the best products have three important areas: 1) solve a problem, 2) be easy to explain and demonstrate, and 3) have mass appeal. I defiantly had all three.

30 MARKETING MY IDEA

I started investigating Edison Nation and wondering if that's the way to go. If they are partnered with Daymond John, they are definitely a reputable company. So I joined their program and submitted my idea to what would be an eight-step process including prescreening and review, IP research, design stages and various considerations, and the final review, all before it would be selected to go to market. It would be another long road, but in my mind would be very well worth it.

I cannot remember exactly but the search was for a specific industry, and I submitted anyway and participated in weekly member meetings, joined their community to meet other entrepreneurs. It was a very neat program and experience. I remember checking my status daily to see if it would move to the next level and reading threads from other inventors who would announce they struck a deal. With all this excitement and anticipation I remember one day checking only to find we had a red x. This meant we would no longer go any further in the process and that we are not going to be considered.

So imagine how this would feel. I'm new at this, already having a hard gaining acceptance from salon owners, now this. Most people would quit and I wanted to, but something told me not to. I had learned so much about never giving up and that the best ideas are not easy. All I could think about was my friends' fingers getting cut and how that shouldn't be how it's got to be. I kept moving and I did go through a period of non-activity and losing interest or at least not putting in extra effort.

I figured hey I have a job at Prairie Tech, and I need to focus on that, and the website is not going away and so I can leave it up and just see what happens. I did try to get some of the alliance partners involved but it was so early on that it didn't appeal to them even after they heard my excitement.

It was early 2012, nearing spring, and I got a call from Edison Nation and it was the magazine division called *Inventors Magazine*. They wanted to feature Cosmo Finger Guard in the May 2012 issue along with some other new products; it was definitely an uplifting boost that was needed and great timing.

Of course, I would want to have my product featured in it so we did and it came and went and it was one of those temporary rushes, like making a sale and then figuring out I now have to go out and sell again. The rush is over and things started to slow again, and for about the next eight months there was almost no activity, slow sales, no marketing on my part, and now I am back focusing heavily on my business development for Prairie Tech.

I mean I can't let both slow down, so this gave me an incentive to do well on technology sales, and I even got to the point—I cannot believe I was going to do this—where I was ready to shut it down and turn off the website. I had spent all the money I could on developing it, patents, attorney fees, and manufacturing, and had had about all I could do with it.

So the idea was there but getting no traction, and one of the members from Prairie Tech approached me after hearing I was going to shut it off and he asked what needed to be done. Honestly it was just the need for more money and an investment. So Troy, who is now a business partner, owner, and investor decided to get involved, and after a few meetings we came to the conclusion that we needed to keep the website on, get some inventory, and do a little social media marketing, so we did.

It was very refreshing and was again another period in time that now looking back is absolutely proof that you should never give up. And even though I would have shut the website off, I still had a patent filed and pending so it wasn't like I would have lost anything and I could have fired it up again later when I was ready. But it would have looked bad to the consumers who had already purchased the product as well as to anyone who I previously had approached with how great of an idea it was. This would have certainly made me look bad as well. I was pretty happy and very thankful that he wanted to invest and it was exactly what we needed.

A lot of people knew I had this product and he was the only one who stepped forward. I cannot say that that everyone I know should have helped because that is unfair, but I know some who wished they had, and I am in no way upset and I completely understand. I mean let's be honest, I haven't invested in anyone else's dream or idea. So what have I learned here so far, you might ask? I've learned to never give up on your idea and remember you can always find a way. And even though I had felt like giving in, it is still unknown as to the direction things would have went. I know now how important it is. Remember the Will Smith story; this fits in with that perfectly. Here is a new quote to consider at this junction of my book.

"I have not failed. I've just found 10,000 ways that won't work." - Thomas A. Edison

31 THE POWER OF SOCIAL MEDIA

In this new time of inventing, remember that I still have to sell, and I still have to make a living. I was seeing on TV, with the Shark Tank show, that the millionaires and billionaires would all say to inventors trying to get an investment that what they want to see is that you are all in and that you live and breathe your product. I felt I had demonstrated this, but I still also have to make a living and pay my bills.

I continued to focus hard on my business development side for the tech group and was still enjoying great success there, and maybe the turn down on the glove development boosted me. Looking back, it's weird how things happen; it all make sense even though back then it didn't.

I believe I was never meant to take the Cosmo Finger Guard Journey alone and I also believe it was very important to me life's journey, writing this book, and positioning myself to become a KPI is all part of it. I smile now as I write because it is all unexplainable in my mind.

Let me get back to the power of social media now. After Troy came on board we still encountered a slow period with slow sales growth. Then one day in January 2014 I received a call from Fred, the website designer, and he asked me what was going on with the Cosmo Finger Guard website, and I said, "I have no idea what you are talking about." He said you're getting orders left and right, and he was just letting me know I might want to look into this.

I checked my email and sure enough we have dozens and dozens of orders all at once and I had no idea either what was going on until I received a Facebook notice that someone had tagged me in and it was there I could see that a big company, the largest beauty magazine in the world *BehindTheChair.com* had posted a picture on their Facebook page of our glove they found from a customer's post on Pinterest and they asked their online community of followers this question: "Has Anybody Seen This?"

Well BehindTheChair.com's Facebook page had almost a half a million followers all from the beauty industry, and that triggered a boatload of interested hairstylists to order one from our site. We literally sold out and I called my partner Troy and told him about the excitement and that we better order more gloves ASAP. We both laughed and were absolutely amazed.

I remember thanking God for this blessing. Just one picture on the internet put us on the map. There were over 10,000 views, 4,600 shares, and over 1,200 comments just from this one picture. I could not believe it and started to read all the comments. It was like our very own think tank or free customer evaluation.

The comments certainly validated some of the things we already learned and that some comments were asking "where the product had been" and "oh my god we love it" and "how do I order one" to the complete opposite of "this is silly" and "I would never wear that," etc. It went on and on, back and forth; it was a good debate among believers and non-believers.

We had already learned most of what was written so it did not surprise us, and we are grateful of all the comments so we can keep learning. Let's face it, we are new, and no one has ever been trained or asked to wear anything on their hands or fingers, and the veterans of the trade are proud of the scars from finger cuts. Not all of them, but a lot. There was still a large group of reactive buyers who probably wouldn't wear anything either right up to the point where they have an accident and severely cut their finger or take a chunk out of their knuckle.

These stylists are still to this day a large part of our orders— we call them reactive buyers. Then we also have the young and new generation of stylists who are impressionable, like new things, and especially trendy items. This group buys out of curiosity.

To this day, you can find the very post I am talking about on the internet because it has its own link just Google Cosmo Finger Guard on BehindTheChair.com and the link will pop up and you will be able to see what put us on the map and made history.

I have thanked BTC for the post and had even tried to arrange a face-to-face meeting as a follow-up to see if we could work together. But when it comes to my sales skills, follow-up system to set meetings, I was able to get them to reply and they asked me to send samples and we did.

I let time go by and after more follow-up we submitted pricing and this is the point where we lost them. We didn't have enough margins for them to play in the distribution so it was a huge learning lesson and I will talk about that later in the story. In the world of retail and distribution, everyone wants 100% markup and you have to price it that way.

32 REBRANDING

After the Facebook post, we decided it's time to step up to the plate and create our own action by deciding to exhibit in the largest beauty show in North America, the Americas Beauty Show in Chicago. This show was in March that year and was only a few months away and would require us to rebrand our look and image. So we hired our web design and marketing friends to help create a company brochure, a tradeshow display, business cards, and new envelopes.

This is not the type of show to just show up with a banner and wing it. It's a huge expense and needs a lot of inventory and packaging, and all of this has to be crated and ordered in two months, but somehow we made it. We were able to get it all done literally the week of the show and it was an amazing event, and we learned a lot. It was nonstop selling at the booth with an expected 65,000 in attendance in three days.

We gathered as many friends together as we could, and we all had roles just like in grand opening of a store. One would hand out information, another would present the product, another person would try to close the deal, another would charge the customer for the glove, then another would take their picture for social media, and another would scan their badge for follow-up information and for our future email list.

It was nonstop for three days, and although it sound like we should have sold thousands it was impossible. We are a new product, so everyone would want to learn what they could about the Cosmo Finger Guard, try it on, and some would even think about it and come back later. This is all part of the selling process, so we started to get creative with discount offers and my partner, Troy, decided he would present to groups instead of one or two at a time, and he would attract them by showing the use of shears against his hand while wearing the glove.

This would attract anyone's attention because they all knew what would happen to your fingers otherwise; it would cut them up. This seemed to work and we had a great turnout, but it still takes time. Plus you cannot get to everyone, there was just way to many people. So we learned a lot and everyone did their part in helping, and it was a true sales team experience and the first tradeshow of this magnitude. Even for me the things I learned are priceless. I feel you can apply sales to any situation but you have to be creative in an environment like that where there is so much going on and a lot of distractions to pull your potential clients away. The shock and awe of shears was the trick.

33 SHARPENING PRESENTATION SKILLS

I had already started going to a weekly event called *1 Million Cups* before the tradeshow. *1 Million Cups* is a group of entrepreneurs who meet every week all over the United States, and some other countries, to listen to a startup present his or her new idea and receive feedback from the audience while sharpening your presentation skills.

I was very interested in the group and started attending consistently. It was another great learning experience and I would recommend this to anyone, even if you're not a startup and in business development or sales like I am sure a lot of you are.

You can meet a lot of local business people and investors, and each startup may eventually need your service, so it couldn't hurt. There are more of these types of groups available now, so check one out. The group I attended was almost brand new and had only been up and going for a few months before I came on board. I learned something from every presenter, and it also confirmed a lot of things I was already doing. I also found that I wasn't alone in the quest for entrepreneurship. There were people coming out of the woodwork, and heck I've been in business before, many times, and now have a new product so I can probably share some of my experiences since you are able to give feedback.

I was eventually asked if I would present my Cosmo Finger Guard idea, and like I said, this was before the March 2014 Chicago Tradeshow. I was very interested but wanted to wait until I had the show behind me because I knew it would allow me to present another new milestone with my product venture.

I really started to get involved and started promoting the event pretty heavily, and my business development instincts kicked in so I started inviting others to attend to get more people rallied around this new idea.

As if I didn't already know, I like to be involved with new ideas. Here was another one, and now it's a place where I can show off my own product. The people running it became friends and business acquaintances, and they were doing a great job, but I knew I could help and no one needed to ask me to because I was already enthusiastic about the program. You see the idea of the pitch is to sharpen your presentation skills at home in on a six-minute pitch that you can use for an investor. The Kaufmann Foundation in Kansas City started it.

I eventually agreed to present at *1 Million Cups* and the *Americas Beauty Show* in Chicago was a success and had passed, and it's now April 2014. So I invited all my friends and coworkers from Prairie Technology Alliance and I remember thinking wow we have a pretty good-sized turnout. I felt it is one of the best even though it was already growing. I was also sharing the morning with a larger company and that definitely had an impact as well.

In fact, they had attracted the local TV media, but it wasn't for me. I nonetheless ended up getting in a small part.

Another thing I forgot to mention to everyone about getting involved with a group like this, if you have an idea, is that because most, if not all, of the cities participating have a videographer there, your presentation will be taped.

So how cool is that, and in Peoria, IL they will even give you a separate 30-second business card video that you can use, and this is huge to any startup. You can see mine; just Google my name, John McKee, Cosmo Finger Guard, and *1 Million Cups* and they will show up or visit the Cosmo Finger Guard YouTube channel.

I did my presentation and it went long, I think the Q/A took me out to around 45 minutes in all and it was fun. I found a renewed interest and liking to being on stage. I've never told anyone this but, I enjoy it, especially if it's a topic I know inside and out.

Back in my early years at Motorola I used to have to stay late to attend and present to volunteer fire departments to sell paging and two-way radio systems, and I remember that I would have to take the floor in front of all the firefighters, board members, and decision makers. It never seemed to bother me at all, and I later presented more and more and would look for as many opportunities as I could. Looking back, it probably prepared me for the stage, and I look forward to many more similar opportunities.

After presenting and sharpening my skills in Peoria I was eventually asked if I wanted to join the 1 Million Cups Peoria team and volunteer as a Community Organizer. I am sure you don't need me to tell you how excited I was; I took the role without hesitation.

The timing was good. I was an inventor and was in business development and I still had no idea I would be writing soon. I was able to get on board in time for the annual boot camp for 1 Million Cups they hold each year for new organizers in Kansas City. Plus I wanted to apply to speak in Kansas City since it was a much larger stage and audience with major exposure. I cannot remember as I sit here as to whether I presented in Kansas City before or after I went to the boot camp but I ended up doing both.

This was the largest group I have ever presented in front of in my life, which happened in August 2014. I believe we had about 250 people in attendance, and I remember after the event my Twitter account having about 80 twitter notifications from tweets, re-tweets, and likes. The feedback that I got what amazing and I learned once again I felt very comfortable on stage. It's also available on Google if you want to check it out.

The networking opportunity was also very valuable and the connections I made that day helped me in so many ways. I later applied to two more 1 Million Cups events. Eventually I spoke on stage in Cedar Rapids, IA and Des Moines, IA for a total of four events before I hung up my hat. I even took my partner, Troy, to the Des Moines event and my girlfriend, Betty, joined me and supported me in Kansas City.

I look back at that time and I feel I was always learning more and more about the importance of branding myself, but I didn't know I would. I recently read a quote by Grand Cardone:

"If you're not willing to Promote Yourself Then Why Should Anyone Else."

During my time as a Community Organizer at 1 Million Cups, I was back to using my business development skills and started filling my prospecting funnel with startup candidates. See how you can use these skills in just about anything you do.

I know I am good at it, but I do not tell people or act arrogant; it's all in my mind. I believe you have to think it and know it, and then you will do it. For me, the more and more I write, the more I can't wait to finish this. The 1 Million Cups experience was another opportunity in my mind to learn and showcase my skills, but for the first time to show that I care to give back to the community and to other startups in the community.

I am sure I can ask the team there now how many I signed up, but I know it was a lot, even including a few from my own circle and one from Prairie Technology Alliance. I love showcasing other businesses and helping them get additional exposure and opportunities to tell their stories. The audience grew and grew. I would get there first thing in the morning before anyone else, if I could, and start setting up, arranging the chairs, putting up signs, and meeting with presenters to discuss their presentations. I would also find ways tell them this is your day. This morning is all about you, so enjoy it and when it's all said and done you will even have a new video to watch yourself and hone in on your skills. It's hard for me to explain how much excitement I got from the light being shined on another local startup. "There is nothing more rewarding than giving back and expecting nothing in return"

I did this for nine months and was there every Wednesday of every week sharing my experience and learning from each and everyone. Thank you to all the people who I worked with during that time. The boot camp in Kansas City was also amazing, it was designed for all new community organizers and we had around 100 from all over the country.

The training was to develop best practices and to discuss new ideas and what the future of 1 Million Cups looked like. Many of us have moved on and many new faces are onboard today, as they typically rotate out organizers at around nine months to keep everything fresh. If you ever want to speak in front of an investor or group, I encourage anyone to look into this program, and there are many others available just like it.

34 GIVING BACK

I have always had the desire to give back to my community and have always served in some type of volunteer position, and even though I didn't look at it as something I do well, it wasn't until 1 Million Cups that I realized giving back can also become a passion if it ties into your life somehow or is something that has an effect on you or someone in your life.

The pleasure of giving back is hard to explain until you try it. For me, it's about knowing I am helping someone or some place and I am asking for nothing in return. Prior to 1 Million Cups, I was active at a major local hospital for over a year, spent about the same time giving my time to my local church, at many other community fundraisers and events, and by serving on committees. Now, I feel I really found a good home for me to serve and I am not sure how I've missed it all these years anyway, and I am now at Score Mentors.

Score is a national nonprofit association dedicated to helping small businesses get off the ground, grow, and achieve their goals through education and mentorship. Sounds great right?

It is and I love it. I wish I had more time to offer support. I do what I can and have been a volunteer here now for a year. I bring this up because not only am I learning from other mentors in many areas of business, I am also able to recruit new volunteers and use my sales and business skills to help others.

My latest offering was to present a workshop on "Prospecting for Sales" subtitled "Nothing Happens until the Meeting is Set". Hence the subtitle and end focus of this book. It helped me put my own puzzle together, understand my niche, and it's definitely helping me standout as an expert in sales, meetings, and business development.

I also enjoy teaching and sharing my knowledge. In fact, my Score workshop was recorded as one of the largest workshop turnouts in Peoria's Chapter, resulting in the demand for more, and quoted and written as a recommendation by the Chapter Chair on my LinkedIn profile. My point and opinion, here, is that you have to look back to put all the pieces together for it to make sense and to see all the dots connecting before you can determine what you want to focus on as a Key Influencer.

35 PRODUCT EVOLUTION

I want to get back to the product development now and bring you up to speed on the journey to https://asseenontv.pro/ and meeting Kevin Harrington from Shark Tank and TV infomercials.

I left off earlier with the success of the first national tradeshow, the 1 Million Cups speaking engagements, and getting exposure on BehindTheChair.com. Now we are entered into a new contest on Edison Nation for another round. However, this time it's for an open search to find new products, and we are doing well. Weeks and months are going by and we move from step one all the way to the final step, step eight. We are even now getting calls about conversations with CVS and Walgreens, etc. To this day I'm not sure why, but I started looking into the agreement which I should have done in the beginning. I found out we would have to do some type of transfer agreement, and I didn't want to do that, so I pulled the plug.

I feel bad because I like Edison Nation, I trust them, and I'm still a member to this day. So it wasn't anything they did at all, I just did not read the fine print regarding patents. I still socialize with Edison Nation and would recommend them to anyone.

It was all me, and I called my partner and told him what I was doing. So now what? I pulled the Cosmo Glove form the search and felt we could make a deal happen on our own. I am confident and maybe the search was the confidence booster I needed. I did not get much of a chance to do anything else and a year passes by, and the whole time I am working hard on social media, getting exposure, exhibiting more tradeshows, and in fact that particular year we went to a Des Moines, IA beauty show, and Evansville, Indiana beauty show, and we exhibited again in the Americas Beauty show. Along with my business development role for Prairie Technology Alliance, we remained busy. I was full speed ahead.

During this period we sharpened our skills with pitching the glove at the tradeshows, started making amateur videos, and designed two more gloves for our product lineup based on customers' feedback. Then we filed two more patents and just kept firing away at opportunities.

We had orders coming from the United Kingdom, Australia, Canada, and all over the country; nothing overwhelming, but we were happy with the acceptance and slow movement, because we knew we are creating the market ourselves. I've learned from other successful entrepreneurs to keep going no matter what the success is because if you believe in it, despite the odds, do it anyway.

A great quote I just read today is by the CEO of Tesla, Elon Musk. He says, "If something is important enough even if the odds are against you, YOU SHOULD STILL DO IT." See, we are not taking sales from another market, because the product we sell does not exist, we are creating the market. So, the difference between us or anyone else inventing is that not only have we created a new product, we are also creating the market and paving the way for ourselves and possibly for others down the road who may follow us after we get their attention.

I started contacting the beauty schools again. After a lot of rejection, I focused on the ones we could drive to and offered a demonstration of our product, and by doing so I was able to secure the meetings. This should be no surprise, since this is still really what I do, even though I still haven't realized the value of my skill set in connecting people, business, and product.

Remember, I am back in time now, and this period is before the meetings with Kevin Harrington, reading his book, and the light bulb going off. It is what is natural to me, and even still, at this time I kept setting meetings for Prairie Tech Alliance. I do my homework on who the contacts are, start with my email introductions, follow-up, and use the convincing style that I have.

None of these are hard sells, they are soft sales. But I finally get my first appointment at Empire Beauty School in Chicago, and we are given access to the students and 30 minutes to present the glove's history, provide a demonstration, and then make the sale. It was a great feeling of accomplishment once again. I am addicted to cranking though making meetings happen. It's so natural to me, and in my opinion it's easy. But you know, my motto is: nothing ever happens until the meeting is set.

After the first meeting and demonstration, I then go through the process again and replicate what I did the first time. Only the second time is easier, because now I have a contact or referral from the first meeting that I use to drop their name, and now I am on a roll. I duplicate the same process again, again, and again until I've now presented at every Empire

Beauty School in Chicago. My plans were to then use this information and approach Empire Beauty School's corporate office.

I am doing all these activities while cranking out meetings for Prairie Tech, and something has a hold of me now; I am feeling like I am on fire and I am so motivated. It's hard to explain. During the tradeshow in Evansville, Indiana I was able to meet Tabatha Coffeey, and if anyone knows anything about the beauty industry, you will know that she is the queen of reality TV for the beauty industry.

She has a series on Bravo TV called "Tabatha Takes Over". She was doing a book signing, so I purchased a book and found her in the hallway and approached her for a photo. She accommodated me. Then later I saw her again for the actual book signing. She signed my book and we had another fantastic photo opportunity.

But my partner went one step further than me. Instead of having her sign a book, he asked her to sign a pink Cosmo Finger Guard. How cool is that. Had we been thinking we should have had her name embroidered on some and given her a few.

Well, I have to be honest here, I had done that early on in the inventing process, and after that we had them made. I did have her name put on them and sent them to her management team. I have no idea to this day if she even received them. It's funny because this is all a few years later when we actually get to meet her. It was so real and maybe I will get lucky and she will read my book and remember me as the glove inventor guy.

36 LEARNING ABOUT OUR CUSTOMERS

So, as you can see, I was busy and this was all part of the learning curve for creating a product. I know in my mind that I am not giving up and we have to blaze a trail, and gain acceptance, and create a brand no matter how slow the process is and no matter how long it takes. In my mind, as long as we are making sales, and as long as people keep buying the glove, it's confirming that there is a market.

We just need to be patient, and we also know that we are dealing with a generation change. So what am I talking about; well I'm learning that the veterans of the hairdressing world are split. We have those that say if you're cutting your fingers then you shouldn't be in the business, as well as those who do cut themselves and they are proud of their battle wounds.

This generation will buy and are also very reactive, but hesitant because they've never seen our glove, have never heard of it, and no one was ever trained with it. That makes perfect sense to us, and 90% of our sales up to this point are reactive buyers.

Then there is the next generation, the ones who are still in Cosmetology and Beauty School. This is the group I mentioned earlier when we were touring the beauty schools in Chicago. When we would go there, we would sell, and the excitement was contagious from that group.

They are all impressionable, love fashion, and really do not want to get cut at work; I mean who would. So this tells us it's just a matter of time, exposure, and availability. We also know that the big names in the beauty industry have to eventually accept the glove as a safety item as well and we just need to keep selling, keep marketing, keep attending tradeshows, keep educating the next generation, and keep making it fun.

By fun I mean, let's get them involved. So when we exhibit at a tradeshow and a customer visits, we take their picture and post it on our social media sites. I know we are not the first to do this, but I guarantee you we are creating images of belief. We are not only capturing great moments in history, we are also creating real proof to any onlookers of the larger picture who cannot dispute what we have done, and that people are interested and curious about safety. I have hundreds of photos with clients, and it's important to us as well because we are a web-based business, and not available in beauty stores yet, and so we do not get to see and talk with our customers, so the tradeshows are so exciting. It's also an opportunity to learn from customers what they like and dislike and from that we have created two more versions of our Cosmetology glove and have those patents pending.

37 ASSEENONTV OPPORTUNITY

There is no dispute in our minds that there should be a safety concern within the beauty industry. We are excited each day that goes by, and we gain more traction, and someday gaining full industry acceptance will be a sweet feeling.

As we get closer and closer to the latest year, we just keep on selling, making calls, pushing out social media, and we even garner some additional magazine coverage and start discussing opportunities all over the world. Then one day around October or November of 2015, we received an email from the Studios of AsSeenOnTv.Pro in Coral Spring Fla., wanting us to participate as a strategic partner in TV Infomercials with Kevin Harrington.

We are excited, and we schedule several calls with them and even arrange a meeting in Florida for early December. By this time we have already entered into an agreement to partner up, and this will be my first visit to meet Kevin Harrington.

In the meantime, I am able to start talking about it all, and I am starting to get excited about new possibilities for marketing. I know by now that everything I have learned has happened for a reason, and this is an opportunity to get exposure using the name of AsSeenOnTV.Pro and Kevin Harrington.

I have to get all the marketing materials approved before sending anything out, but I am thinking press releases, social media, and local media. I finally arrive in Florida in December 2015, and it's a one-day session where I and other entrepreneurs with ideas and products come together for a presentation by Kevin and one-on-one mentor time.

The next morning after my arrival, I had already arranged a visit to the studios and met with my contacts, the business development department, and the V.P. At the studios, I get a quick tour to meet producers, scriptwriters, etc., and then unexpectedly I meet Kevin in the hallway. It's a pretty cool opportunity for me knowing what I have been through, and I would have never thought that I would meet him or any Shark from TV in person. I was actually pretty calm, though, despite it not actually being a planned meeting. Our first meeting was supposed to be later at the Innovators Think Tank with all the rest of the inventors. You can understand why I was feeling a bit special at that moment. So we exchanged a few words and then we had to get going to finish the tour and let Kevin get back to his schedule.

Later that morning we finally all met and we are all re-introduced to the studio team and Mr. Harrington. He gave a wonderful presentation, and I remember listening intently to what he had to say. I mean he is the king of infomercials, has sold billions in sales for hundreds of products, from the early days of the knives, grills, and washing supplies, to everything else in between. And here I was soaking it all up. I remember him talking about the five key elements of success, and the two most important things that stood out to me was raising my profile and writing a book.

I remembered it and started thinking: Can I do this? Am I able to raise my profile and write a book, and if I do write a book, what would it be about? Would it be about inventing my Cosmo Finger Guard or a life story or about sales? I mean this is all a brand new turn for me, meaning, I have been in sales and business development all my life, and all of a sudden I am at an innovators think tank listening to a Shark Tank investor. It's all just so amazing how it can transform so quickly, and I am starting to realize the value of everything around me: my invention, my business development skills, and the way my profile is changing, etc.

It is also an opportunity for me to do what I know best and that's to network with other inventors and get to know them, because connections are becoming so much more important to me these days, you just never know who or what you may need. After Kevin is done with his presentation, we each get to spend about ten minutes with him one-on-one, and then we are able to take pictures. The one-on-one time was great, and I remember him giving me advice and ideas to use to help with the continued success or the Cosmo Finger Guard.

I honestly wasn't expecting anything grand, so I was surprised when he offered me his email address to do a few follow-ups with him after the event. I honestly didn't fully understand the gravity of the opportunity. Although I brought him samples, I should have brought shears or succors to demonstrate, but I didn't know if I could or that's how it would be.

So nonetheless, it was still a fantastic opportunity and I learned a great deal, and also learned to be ready for a pitch opportunity. Now I create my own quotes about being prepared and post them on social media so others can be ready, and honestly, the ironic thing about it is was that I had been to four 1 Million Cups events where you get six minutes to tell your story. So I fault myself for that one, but I could tell he still saw the value in the product as a solution to a problem, it's easy to explain how to use, and it can be sold to the masses.

It's also so very interesting looking back to those moments, because I have now read his book on becoming a KPI and one of the lessons I've had to learn is to craft my introduction after meeting him so that I am able to tell a compelling story and be a vital contributor. Not to have a simple reply or simple story like I am in business development or that I created a glove or even that I may have been a business manager, store operator, business owner, etc, etc. Here is what I am talking about and what a crafted pitch of you and your niche should sound like when someone asks you what you do:

"I specialize in connecting people, business, and products through paid arranged meetings using my own proven system, which will save you time, money, and lower your cost per meeting. Is there a business you would like to meet with or do you have a product you would like to launch? I can help."

At the age of 53, I get it: I get the importance of being a vital contributor in my specialized area of expertise. And even though I just invented a really cool product that will be introduced by a shark and could turn that into some type of area of expertise, it's really not. Inventing a specialty glove is a byproduct of me being a true-blooded entrepreneur and wanting to always be creating and always being onto the next adventure.

My whole life up to this point has been a series of trying something new and not settling down and working nine to five for a living. I want to create my own way, and I am now seeing that all of this is starting to make sense to me now, but it hasn't arrived yet. But I am getting ahead of myself already. Let's get back to the product development and AsSeenOnTV.Pro opportunity.

So, with the event behind me, and now headed back home, my head is spinning again and I'm thinking of all the ideas I have to blow this up and make a larger deal out of it for myself and for the company and product. I immediately started planning to write press releases, order new banners for tradeshows with Kevin's picture on it, and increase social media announcing our plans to be on TV, and the list goes on.

The writing of the script is next along with gathering all my participants to put an infomercial together. I need someone to be in the hair scene. I need a professional salon. Since we have also now launched new gloves, we will also need a chef and someone in culinary. Finally, I'll need locations for all the shoots.

I'm busy putting all of these things together and time is of the essence. On top of this new opportunity I have two beauty tradeshows coming up in January and March of 2016. It's now already early January 2016 and I have my plate full. I'm feeling real good about it all and I manage to get it all lined up for the one-day video shoot. I am also able to get myself landed in the January issue of IBI Magazine, a local business issue popular in our area.

They did an interview about the Cosmo Finger Guard and because AsSeenOnTV.Pro was coming to town. Next, the local CBS Fox News Channel Affiliate interviewed me for the same thing, and that aired in February. We were able to squeeze in a smaller tradeshow in Des Moines, IA during all of this and I am just soaking it all up. I have never had so much attention and I admit I love it.

I use it all and push it through all our social media outlets such as Facebook, Twitter, Instagram, YouTube and Pinterest, and I'm starting to realize how very important it all is and it's not going to last forever, and if I'm going to want to keep this lifestyle I'm going to need to do something about it. You only live once, and I'm 53 years old. Why did I wait so long? This is why I believe everything is about timing and knowing when your ship has arrived. I am sure I could have done all of this earlier in life, but I couldn't predict that. All I can do is put the pieces together now and make the best of what I have left.

38 A TURNING POINT IN MY LIFE

It's now February, and it's time to pick up a copy of a book called "Key Person of Influence" from a tweet I saw from Mr. Harrington. I impulse shopped and ordered it right on the spot. Once it arrived, I was able to read it in a week, and after I was done I was so pumped at what I had learned, and it simply reinforced what I heard at the Innovators Think Tank in early December. However, there was an additional element to it I clearly had not thought too much about and that's how to take what you already know and turn it into a niche of whatever it is I am good at.

See when I first started writing I was intending on writing about the whole inventing process because that is what got me all the press, and meeting people and the star feeling and I did do exactly that. I can now honestly tell all of you I've changed my focus from inventing to what I know the most about and that's business development and arranging paid meetings. I remember even sending Mr. Harrington an email before even buying the book talking about my experience and how I could even help them.

Isn't that funny? Me helping them, like they need my help! That's not what I really meant, and I know they do not need me, and I was just referring to my wealth of contacts and ability to search out and find new products. I love to do what I do, and I am always trying to help.

Let's not forget I'm still at Prairie Tech, and I'm still contracted to serve the group of local technology companies. I owe the group top-notch high-end business-to-business service because it's enabled, me to keep developing my glove, and they have been the absolute best people I have ever worked for in my life. They know I have a new product and, as previously discussed, one became a partner and investor early on in 2014 and another one has done the same just here recently in 2016.

So without them, none of this would be possible. This also gives me an opportunity to thank all of them, especially Troy and Kevin, for seeing the same vision I do and moving forward with me.

The KPI book honestly has already changed me. Now I am focused on what my real niche is. Even though I am clearly capable of inventing my craft in arranging meetings. I've done it for every single place I've worked, and so this enables me to say I am an expert at setting meetings, and towards the end of the book I'll finally share my system and the processes I use still to this day. But becoming a KPI is still not going to happen overnight, and I'm still not done sharing my inventing story because there moments in recent time that I still feel are relevant in aid to my desire to be the very best at my craft.

39 HELPING OTHERS

I have been involved with other inventors and had the desire to help them as well, one of which is also in the beauty industry and has manufactured their own professional shampoo line. I wanted to help them with the same process we experienced with the TV opportunity, and so I put my contacts together and arranged a meeting for them to speak with the TV Studio, and they are working through it.

I also meet weekly with another inventor for lunch and we discuss ways to help each other with our products. It is a new passion I have. I've always wanted to give back, and I do on a regular basis through volunteering at the local Score Mentors chapter in Peoria.

It's now March 2016, and it's time to exhibit in the Americas Beauty Show once again. It's even more exciting this time, because we have the approval to market as an AsSeenOnTV.Pro product, and use the logos and the Kevin Harrington images.

I am taking full advantage of the social media and even told the social media department for Americas Beauty Show that we challenge all the other exhibitors to try and do more coverage than us on social media. We sent out information every day for the month of March leading up to the event taking place on the 22nd. We are not only getting noticed, but orders are becoming more frequent, and we are just having absolute fun.

The show finally arrives and we are flooded with opportunities like no other time. We have three groups in the show that want to interact with us, and we are just blown away. This is all adding to my star feeling that I'm starting to get. I'm not a star, but I think if you feel and act in a certain way, you will be what you want.

I am in no way shape or form that kind of person, but because I'm not, most will think I am because they've not seen that side of me. I sincerely appreciate everything everyone has done for me and will be indebted to them all forever, because without the supporters I wouldn't have made it this far, and they all know whom they are. It's the same people I referenced earlier in this book and I hope they know from the bottom of my heart no matter how successful I ever become, I am never too big or too much for them.

Now, that that's behind us I need to stay focused on bringing this story full circle. It's all becoming clear for me what my next hurdle is. I run into another product developer at the Americas Beauty Show who approached me and wanted to talk about our journey, how we got to the point of being in a big show like this, and how we got investors, and how we became partners with AsSeenOnTV.Pro.

I want to help, but I can't help everyone for free. I would if I could, however, so this got me thinking about the whole learning to become a KPI and arranging meetings and using my skills to help others. It's becoming clearer and clearer each and every day that I feel my new mission is to help others be successful and then it will translate into me becoming more successful.

I'm watching and studying as many successful mentors as possible and learning their systems. I will be honest, in areas, no matter what anyone is doing—creating, inventing, or building a new business—they all need business development and growth in sales, and to make connections, appointments, and meetings happen. That's my real skill, and that's the area I will be focusing on. And when you read the final pages on how it's done you may say that's a great idea, or you may say I can do it better, and I say more power to you.

When we finally get the camera crew ready to film, I had done all the calls and set up all the meetings I could to make the filming run smoothly. I arranged all the filming locations, the cast, and crew and the film date arrived, and it was lights camera action. You can see pictures from the film date on our Cosmo Finger Guard Facebook Page and some on my personal page as well if you search back to February 2, 2016, as well as on Twitter @CosmoGlove, and the final 60-second infomercial that has Kevin Harrington introducing us is on our Facebook page as well and on our YouTube page.

Our infomercial features an award winning salon from *Salon Today* magazine featured called Five Senses Salon and Spa, and we have a special appearance from Shark Tank alum Dave Alwan of Echo Valley Meat appear in the infomercial, as well as a local prominent chef. We are so lucky to have all of them, and it was great to get them involved. The film day went smooth and it was a success and we expect to start airing the TV infomercials all over the U.S. starting April 2016.

This is all so too real, and I sometimes don't even think about it because that's how my mind works. I read a great article recently about never living a boring life on Entreprenuer.com, and it references why you should never just start one business. If you're going to be an entrepreneur, those who start more than one business will never lead a boring life. Although I have to admit, I've had plenty of boring times in my life, I look back and think to myself that I wasn't working on more than one business idea at the time to keep me on track.

Life happens and I would easily get off track, and now that time is running out, I am more focused than ever. I also admit I'm a bit scared because it's a new territory for me. Not the starting a new business part, but really going after a much, much larger picture, and put myself out there as an expert in arranging meetings because at the end of the day that's what this is all about.

It's not about the Cosmo Glove, TV commercials, magazine articles, nor the fortune 500 companies I've worked for or the businesses I've started, it's about what DO I DO BEST. I sell meetings and I'm very good at it. If you're reading this book I'm sure you feel it's such a simple task, and it is, but I'm acting on it. I'm not giving up on anything to do it either. In fact, I want to work harder at it all.

I want to do the very best job for Prairie Technology Alliance, Cosmo Finger Guard, and any new business opportunities that rise from this book or me going public with a new website, social media, press releases, sales meetings appointments, and everything I'll do that I've learned to make it all possible. I assure my readers, I'll go down in a blazing fashion before I give up.

I know I'll have setbacks and I know I'll be ridiculed especially for the arrogance that comes from marketing yourself. But you have to do it, and there is another quote I think of as I'm typing that fits in here right now real well and that's a quote that reads something like, "Work hard now for several years like most won't, so that you will be able to live the rest of your life like most can't."

Another one states, "The ones that will hate you now will be the ones who will ask for a job later." I cannot remember the names of the quotes' authors, but the quotes have stuck with me. Remember I am big on quotes. Someone recently took notice and commented to me on Facebook about my quotes, one of which was sentenced wrong and that was a little embarrassing, so I will need to watch my writing skills. Then a high school friend commented on another quote stating that I must really be into quotes, and I replied saying that as of that date I've been sending out a daily quote Monday through Friday every week for the last seven years. So I definitely know a few. I like knowing that not only can I wake up to something inspirational, but also that I am able to get it into the eyes and minds of my co-workers before their days starts.

40 NEXT STEPS ACTION PLANS FOR KPI

In this section, I write about bringing everything I have learned together. Why becoming a Key Person of Influence in connecting people, businesses, and products is a good fit for me, to solidify to the world my system to find more leads, and to arrange more meetings to do business together. I have covered a lot in this book, from my early days of setting appointments door-to-door for home improvement meetings at night to how acquiring a meeting started just by a click of the mouse, to stay focused and never give up on developing your ideas and evolving business development concepts.

So what's next for John McKee? Well we are starting to air our TV infomercials on networks such as E! Entertainment, Food Network, Cooking Channel, and Lifetime, and things are looking pretty good for the development of my product. We have another new investor who likes the idea and concept. We have some really cool ideas coming up to prepare for the long haul to positioning ourselves as a national brand, and we have even joined a few beauty organizations, where we can start developing our relationships with beauty school owners.

We are positioning ourselves for a movement more than a brand. We have the largest collection of stylists who have been injured using shears. It consists of customers, who have been injured with shears.

We feel extremely confident that our product, Cosmo Finger Guard will be developed into a standard optional safety item that can be used while training. We are for the next generation of stylists and barbers.

We feel the support must come from mentors and key influencers of the beauty industry. To let the students feel comfortable about trying a Cosmo Finger Guard and not let others make them feel bad just because others aren't willing to try. So that covers the product development end.

I've started to really focus hard on building my connections on LinkedIn by adapting to business social selling with relevant content posts, becoming engaged in conversations to give answers and work anniversary reminders; all of this to establish a consistent communication with all my contacts.

I feel cold calling is getting easier now; however, there are still a lot of business owners and contacts who have still not adopted social media, and when I get a chance I try to help encourage the use, but this still tells me cold calling the traditional or old ways is not completely dead no matter what you've read.

These days I almost accept every connection request that comes my way; I've started building a new website for business453.com that I hope to push out to the world very soon and that will help promote the new book and showcase my skills and the services I have to offer as a key influencer in the business-to-business development world, and it will be done when this book is finished.

I'm studying the mentors I follow every single day, watching their videos and reading their posts and articles. As well as being a mentor myself and giving back on every single occasion, I can, and I'm starting to get requests directly and will also use Score. I'll be looking for speaking engagements with a few already lined up that I would have never thought I would be asked to do, and it makes me proud to be able to get the exposure and share my knowledge.

I also attend just about every social event I can within driving distance. I've started my own Twitter account, @JohnMcKee453, and built a new Facebook page for business453, and I'm writing this book. As I said, I hope to have published very soon and announce it all together. It should be pretty exciting, and I hope that everyone reading this is starting to get the larger picture.

Folks, I'm realizing how short life is, and time has become more valuable to me more than ever, and I want to do all that I can. We hear it almost every day and it's true; each day is a new beginning, and you get a chance at a fresh start every single day. Let me assure you, especially the younger generation, please don't wait, get going and get started today, wake up with a new attitude and create your plan of attack on life. Choose a niche and no matter what you do you will succeed if you put in the time and effort.

The business opportunities for me are endless, and they have already started to reach out to me since I've put a few things out there about writing a book on my niche and becoming a KPI.

The launch of my Twitter account has also generated some interest, people asking me questions, wanting to meet, and asking for help. I wish I had launched Twitter earlier because it's such a valuable business tool and I do not usually boast, but I have some rather large influencers following me, so I have to walk the walk now. I will also take a look at new social media like Snapchat and Periscope. The idea is to create my own media outlets.

One is a major contributor on LinkedIn seeking to expand business development, another one who is based out West with ties to the energy market, another who is a product developer who I connected to AsSeenOnTV.pro, and another who has asked me in the past about process management leads. I have not even started to market yet, but I know that I will do extremely well.

I am loyal to Prairie Technology Alliance, and I'm not seeking any opportunities with competitive organizations, I'm just talking about opportunities for help and direction. As a matter of fact, I want to do even more for the alliance group. They are my friends, business partners, and customers.

I've always wanted to do something extraordinary at Prairie Tech, anyway, and one of my ideas was to do reality filming on business meetings and the day-to-day things I go through to find and secure a meeting and what happens at the meeting. Another idea is to interview or Podcast the members and create a regular series. I think both of these ideas would make a pretty cool series, so that might be my next task after I get ramped up. But I will certainly use all of this to help leverage the Alliance in anyway I can. I think this book will help both of us.

My job is not a science, but I've still invested a lifetime into crafting how to do it better and with more enthusiasm. I really enjoy business-to-business sales development, and in my opinion, it's the best job in the world. I have so many tools available now compared to 20 years ago when I didn't even have a mobile phone or even a pager. And today we can do anything we want with technology.

I just watched a Facebook video the other day on Microsoft Research who created and is testing a Holoportation 3D teleportation system in real time, so at some point if I am still around we will be able to put myself in the office of my prospect without leaving home via 3D cameras and audio.

Of course, even then someone will still need to be great at arranging those meetings. Because you're not just going to show up, right?

However, depending on the advancement of the technology, maybe I will. Maybe the teleportation system of the future will allow me to teleport myself right to the office of my cold call and I will pitch what I am offering right there in the lobby as we do today when trying to secure a meeting. It should be very interesting for the next generation of sales and business development professionals.

In any case, and as I was saying, it's not really difficult to be in sales; however, it's not for everyone. And as I sit here and think about the new entrepreneurs I have met in mentor sessions or at group speaking meetings with startups, where I get to listen to amazing ideas, I am wowed how smart most of them are.

However, I am finding that although most startups have great business plans, products, services, or ideas not all have a business development plan. They have a marketing plan but no real mention on what they, as an owner or founder, are going to do to personally secure new clients.

Certainly you hear them reference Facebook, Instagram, Periscope, Skype, and other social media tools, but as of now in this very time I'm just not hearing about sales calls or securing face-to-face meetings even if they are on Skype. It still needs to be done. I am not sure if there are any new studies out yet on the next generation of B2B sales people. But what I do know is available and it helps me build my case even stronger is that the cost of finding, hiring, training, and keeping a professional business rep is extremely expensive.

I'm mean honestly, if I was to ever stop being a business entrepreneur, which would never happen, but if I did, I would be very expensive to recruit. And even if you were able to recruit me with an enticing package, with sign-on bonus, car, expense account, and salary, by time you get me up and going you could have already hired a contract person who offers business development services. Contract sales services will grow in demand. In the time it takes to hire and train a full time representative you probably could have already secured three months' worth of business meetings for much less from a contractor like us. Don't get me wrong, organizations will still always need a direct hire business development or sales person because someone still has to close the sale. But the frontend process of the sales, i.e., finding the prospect and setting up a solid meeting is the most important part. Nothing is ever sold without an initial meeting.

41 THE NEXT GENERATION OF ME

According to UltimateLead.com the average cost of a Business-to-Business sales call in 2001 was about $392. That's $518 in 2013 dollars, including salary, travel, and expenses. That's expensive! And it's now 2016 so we would need to calculate that as well.

It's also a fact that even though social selling has increased sale representatives activity and more and more are closing more deals according to LeadGenius.com, only 59% of sales representatives are expected to achieve his/her quota this year, down from 67% in 2013, that's alarming if you're the company paying their salaries or you are a startup.

These are all good reasons to hear me out on the idea that "Nothing Happens Until The Meeting is Set" and the importance of the proper training for startups and entrepreneurs. I know business sales training is available; however, there is little to no focus on Entrepreneurs.

I have been doing this for over 26 years, and we have always called what I do canvassing, cold calling, or telemarketing. Call it what you want, but you will have to focus at some point on how to acquire the lead and you will have an expense to get the meeting arranged.

Whether you hire a professional business account executive, hire a telemarketing company, or your using social media, someone will still have to confirm the meeting and solidify the date and time. The customer is certainly not just going to send you a message or call, and if they do it's not happening on a regular basis and I'm not talking about retail or selling using ecommerce.

I am talking about a business-to-business meeting to offer a service, product, or solution, and in my case, it may even be a meeting to arrange an introduction. Meaning, what if someone wants to meet an investor and has the greatest idea in the world, but has no sales or cold calling skills.

Or here is another idea I have already mentioned: what about all the entrepreneurs with these great app ideas and all the people with a startup that I've watched at pitch groups who have everything planned but, do not mention anything about how they will sell business to clients. Social Selling is great, but someone has to go to the meeting.

Here is another idea: the number one reoccurring problem I've seen in all of my experiences with every company I have worked for in sales is keeping the representatives. They do very well and outsell the compensation program, then leave because they cannot make any more money.

Another large group will leave and sometimes they are the ones who don't do well and do not meet quotas. Or they are let go after a year or less because they didn't perform. Then the owners and sales managers are back to square one again. This is a huge area for offering a system where you could buy a meeting from a company or a sales contractor like business453.

You could hire someone who knows the lead generating

system and this gives a representative a way to be on their own and become an entrepreneur. If they buy meetings from a company who specializes in arranging them it will save them time, money, and frustration. Let the founder of the business close the deal and solidify the terms and conditions of the sale. This is the part of the sale where you need to know more about the details of the product or service, and most business owners are that knowledgeable.

When most business owners are in front of a qualified prospect, they can get the job done. And for the businesses that do have a business development or sales representative, they can focus on what they do well and that is closing deals.

Remember way back in the beginning of the book when I gave you details about my door-to-door canvassing job I had with the siding and home improvement company? I was the person who sought after the lead and I was the one who made the meeting happen, and then we had the closers come back in and complete the deal.

That's what I am talking about. Some may say, well, then you are canvassing again and maybe so, but it's at a much more professional level with more sophistication than knocking on doors of homeowners offering an estimate. As I said then, and I say it again now, I believe I had the better end of the job and the best part of the sales cycle.

I also believe it's the most important part because you can't sell something to someone who is not listening or not present. A confirmed meeting is worth everything to a company, and every company has something to offer. There are also critical roles that would have to be two separate people. Take, for example, a law firm.

Law firms are big business development seekers and have been for a long time. Many of them took advantage of the yellow pages and dominated that industry, as well as billboards and radio, but acquired clients through effective advertising mediums, and it was expensive. But in the case of a legal firm, you would have to let the trained and certified attorney do the close in the consulting stage. A business development person could not do it unless they are one in the same and have passed the bar. But I still think it's easier to let someone set it up for you and represent your company.

I've been doing this now for seven years, in technology and after inventing my Cosmo Finger Guard, and that led me to meeting Kevin Harrington, which led me to reading his Key Person of Influence book; this is what led me to all these conclusions and to ask myself what is it I really do well and know inside and out and do better than anyone else I know? The answer is arranging business meetings. I think it's a great debate and I welcome the feedback; but at the end of the day I'm already doing it.

I am living, breathing proof, and when I think about all the small businesses and all the new tech startups that I've listened to with amazing enthusiasm, I still do not hear the business development side. This is not true of every startup, and there is no debate at all. I know there are a lot of great startups that have excellent business development skills. Some are just such great ideas the business comes to them. We all want one of those gigs, right?

I feel lucky to have the skill set I've acquired, and it was not given to me. I was destined to figure it out and uncover my skills. I think the best quote I've heard that best explains it was said and written by the latest UFC Feather Weight Champion Connor McGregor. Quote:

"There's no talent here, this is hard work. This is an obsession. Talent does not exist. We are all equals as human beings. You could be anyone if you put in the time. You will reach the top, and that's that. I am not talented. I am obsessed."

Maybe I am obsessed, and I think that's good to have a healthy dose of obsession because I agree with Connor that we are all equals, and the only thing that makes me different is I'm willing to make the effort and put in the time.

This also brings up another important point that is more sensitive to me and many other entrepreneurs who are trying to become a successful Key Person of Influence. This is the fact that the more and more I push myself to brand John McKee on the internet; some people that I know no longer come around or talk with me.

As I stated early on in this book, it just so happens to be that I want to focus on raising my profile. To do this there are steps that have been proven that anyone can take to improve their situation. By doing so it's also a fact and proven that your circle of friends will get smaller and smaller, and to me, that is very unfortunate. It is true that when you start promoting yourself people will view you as arrogant and self-centered. Here is another great quote but I am not sure who wrote it. At the bottom of the quote it shows KushAndWiZoom:

"Your Friends Should Motivate and Inspire You. Your Circle Should Be Well Rounded and Supportive. Keep it Tight. Quality over Quantity, Always".

I have also heard that the people who criticize you will eventually want to work for you if you're successful. All of these are very interesting facts and quotes, and I believe it all to be true.

There are enough successful mentors out there who have been down the road I am taking that I can learn from and realize what the end goal is. I still want to help others and I still remain a Mentor at Score. I meet with entrepreneurs and startups on a regular basis and I always will.

However, I have to focus my time on getting this book done, and there will still be a lot of work left even after it's published. It never stops, and if you want to be successful on your own, you never stop learning and growing. I have always been in favor of promoting the companies I represent through as many channels as I can.

Most of the activities I will mention in my action plan are already things I know and have been doing. I do need to give credit to the KPI book by author Kevin Harrington to actually inspiring me to finally turn that same media focus on myself and come forward as the expert in my niche. I have been a private contractor for seven years now and also developed my own patented product four years ago so when the product came along and Shark Tank hit TV; that's when I started learning how to use social media.

Here is my KPI action plan that I have been talking about throughout this book. I want everyone to know what I have done to become a KPI and give you the steps to follow. These are my simple steps on how I plan to become a KPI:

1) Identify My Niche as an Expertise

2) Publicize Myself and Raise My Profile

3) Perfect my Pitch

4) Surround Myself with Like Minded People

5) Always Give Back

Identify My Niche as an Expert

My niche as an expert is Connecting People, Business, and Product through paid arranged client meetings. You may still ask why is that my niche and how do I claim to be an expert. It is simple: I credit myself with having over 25,000 arranged and confirmed sales meetings in the last 26 years.

I have tens of thousands of hours spent cultivating leads. I have opened several of my own businesses that all required me to find new business clients. I have worked for more than one Fortune 500 company who are known for intense sales training programs. Not to mention that I gained external sales training such as Dale Carnegie, Motorola University, and others. More recently in the last seven years I have focused specifically on my own system to acquire sales meetings during that time I represented Prairie Technology Alliance.

They consist of six separate companies who hired me as a business development specialist to open new doors of opportunities for them through arranged meetings. All of them are listed on my LinkedIn profile, have endorsed me, and I still do contract business development for them today. I look forward to another seven years two or three times over.

Publicize Myself & Raise My Profile

Well this one comes pretty easy because of all the social media that is available today. I already started to brand Prairie Technology Alliance online, and people were already becoming familiar with me in central Illinois. I have made it my mission to uncover every possible lead for the Alliance in seven years. I have attended just about every single social event the area has to offer, which includes all of the Chamber of Commerce locations. We have four in all and recently we have expanded that footprint out to an additional two or three more. I've always been a huge fan of our social media pages. I am one of the few people engaged in using social media in our area when networking with the different Chambers. Some people who will read this may disagree with me. That's just my opinion in what I have seen over the years. Yes others are engaged, and the Chamber staff does an excellent job, I'm just saying I am consistent and make it a point to stand out that we are there.

I started my own Twitter page, building a new website for this book and me. I have recently started promoting myself heavy on my product page for Cosmo Finger Guard, which is something I have never done. I've always given the glory to the product and not necessarily to who invented it. I am changing that for me and for my partners. I also plan on writing press releases when the book is finished and available, creating some videos, lining up speaking engagements and mentor sessions, and arranging everything I can do to raise my profile.

This is all of course in line with becoming more engaged in group discussions on LinkedIn and other blogs, and writing a few of my own posts and giving expert opinions. I will look for workshops and talk about how to generate sales leads and social media.

Perfect My Pitch

As amazing as it will sound, this is definitely new to me; even after all the sales training I have had it was never my thing to do. I am good at introductions on cold calls and I do have a pitch for that, but what I now mean is a pitch for what I do in my niche. I also need one for my product. I regret not creating one for my product because I look back now on the opportunity I had when I was sitting across the table from Kevin Harrington. I did say some things in regards to my CosmoGlove and how we always sell out at tradeshows, but it wasn't like I had perfected a pitch. Although he seemed interested and we are now an AsSeenOnTV.Pro strategic product partner, I know it wasn't a good pitch at all. Now if someone asks me what I do at business453, I can now say with confidence and without hesitation:

"I specialize in connecting people, business, and product through paid arranged meetings using my own proven system that helps StartUps and Entrepreneurs with one of a kind focused business 2 business training."

If I have more time I will extend it a little bit more to this statement:

"I specialize in connecting people, business, and product through paid arranged meetings using my own proven system that helps StartUps and Entrepreneurs with one of a kind focused business 2 business training." Is there a person or business you want to meet?

Nothing Happens Until The Meeting Is Set And No Sale Is Ever Made Without A Meeting -John McKee

business453

* Lead Generation * Arranging Meetings * Prospecting
* Cold Calling *Social Selling * Networking

So it's just one more line at the beginning, and, yes, this part is new for me. I will go into the details of the pitch I use while presenting at Prairie Tech on a cold call, and next I will work on one for Cosmo Finger Guard. My partner came up with one already, and it's not a pitch, but it's a visual pitch, and when we are at tradeshows he will say "Cut Hair?" and they will look and he will be cutting into his fingers while wearing the Cosmo Finger Guard, and right away they get it. They watch with shock and awe, which is pretty neat stuff.

Surround Myself with Like Minded People

This is the last step, and I think it's the hardest. Well, it is not hard, but this is the one I am finding offends others that are in my circle. So when in doubt I have to explain to them, or anyone reading this, that I just want to do more, and so it may seem I am putting myself on a pedestal, but it' s no different than me promoting my business. In your business you put the name out on a regular basis and promote what you do best. This is the same thing. I am the business and I will be promoting what I do best, but in no way shape or form am I trying to offend anyone or have someone delete me, etc.

Honestly I am sure most people reading this will understand I hope when you get a copy it inspires you to write because I am making it sound so easy. He is just writing what is on his mind and what he has done in life, and yes, that is correct, so get to writing and call me if you have any questions about how the process went to get the book published. I would be happy to help or point you in the right direction.

Now I better explain how I plan to surround myself with like-minded people, and honestly, when you do something like this, no matter who you are, you really need to be around people who have done what you are trying to accomplish. In my case it's changed my lifestyle and raised my profile as an expert in my field.

The people who are currently more successful than me because they are at the level I am trying to reach; I hope that makes sense. They are the ones that can help me get to where I want to be. I still need support, and so far my friends on Facebook, Twitter, and LinkedIn have been pretty cool about it when I mention I am writing a book. In fact, several are asking for a copy, and I love that, so thank you for inspiring and supporting me.

Don't we all want that in their life, I do! I have been writing this book since January 2016. I started very lightly. Then I really started hitting the pages and trying to fine-tune things before going to an editor in March and April 2016. Most of my writing has been late at night or late afternoon at local coffee shops. The people I am talking about are people you have heard of on TV, the internet, or social media. If you are in business development or are an entrepreneur, then you will want to follow the same people and do whatever you can to someday to meet them or at least a few of them.

These are people like Kevin Harrington, Daymond John, Grant Cardone, Gary Vaynerchuck and Patrick Bet-David. So you might ask how you surround yourself with these guys? Well, I can't actually do it in person, but every single day since starting this new course of action I have been tuned into one or more of them on social media.

They all produce daily inspirational and educational information, and it is readily available on their social media sites. Nowadays they are becoming more and more willing to share their journeys with the general public, not to mention they have written books on the topic. So when I need inspiration or I need to know something or how to do something, it will be available through one of them; you just have to go look for it.

Some you can subscribe to newsletters or join a club or subscribe to their news feeds. They are always doing live streaming and it can actually take a whole day to keep up with all of them, so you just have to look for whatever it is you're in need of at the time. I also engage in larger events now. I am still attending the local Chamber events, and always will, but I like attending the larger events because there you will find the influencers in specific industries. So for example, this year (2016) I will attend and exhibit at the Americas Beauty Show in Chicago where I met several big names of the beauty trade and have connected with them on LinkedIn and now can call on them and plan on doing so.

I will also attend a large Entrepreneurs Convention in Des Moines, IA, and in July I am attending a larger beauty event in Las Vegas. At each one I plan on making those connections. Also, as my income increases from contract opportunities and when the book is published, I will look for areas to improve from using the author title, and I look forward to that as well. So I think and hope you now get the idea.

I have given all of you my plan, and it's a plan of action you can also try by using the same steps. I do not want to claim to be the expert in raising profiles, but I will soon when it's all said and done, because I am going through the process with traceable milestones, and I will be able share what I learn and my own experience.

Just like my experience knocking on doors for siding leads as a teenager and finding new business leads for the larger companies and later inventing a patented product, raising private capital, crowdfunding, social selling, writing a book, and speaking engagements are all life lessons. If you go through the process you are able to speak on the topic. If you go through the motions, over and over and over again for years then most like you can claim yourself to be an expert. That is what I set out to find—to find my niche and come forward with as a brand and as a company, and then grow it exponentially, which someday I hope to write about again as well.

I set out to find why I had so many different types of jobs and businesses, and even inventing a few times. I wanted to know what it meant for me and what it all adds up to so that I can look for common denominators, repetition, and, more importantly, what is fun and does not feel like work.

What makes me want to get up early without hesitation and work right into the weekend and not say I cannot wait for the weekend? Have you ever said that to yourself or others? "I cannot wait for the weekend." What does that really tell you?

To me it says you cannot wait to get your work over with. Imagine doing something that you enjoy so well you can't wait to get up on Saturday to do some more of it. That's how I am starting to feel. I hope everyone can enjoy the same feeling. It's all a fantastic journey.

Always Give Back

This is the last step in my plan. Giving back comes easy for me. I have talked about not doing it just for the money, and if you are, it is all wrong. For me giving back will drive my success and help make my brand even stronger. So what does giving back mean? To me it is volunteering your time and not expecting anything in return. Here is a great quote I like and want to share on the subject.

"You can have everything in life you want, if you will just help other people get what they want." —Zig Ziglar

I have always tried to do something for others even going back to my days of mowing yards. Even though I was being paid, there was still a certain satisfaction of going the extra mile to help someone who would otherwise struggle.

Maybe trim the fence line as an extra service at no charge. Or maybe deliver a product or service a day early. But the best giving is true giving. I have had the pleasure of helping my local hospital by giving my free time at the emergency room helping check in sick patients. I have helped my local church with ushering congregants to their seats and holiday events. I have given my time to many charities. In the last two years I have specifically given back to the Startup and Entrepreneur community.

I have dedicated my time to 1 Million Cups and helping entrepreneurs prepare their pitch on stage to get feedback before going to an investor. This program also shines the light onto their business and gives them a little bit of social media exposure.

I have been giving my time as a Score Mentor through private one-on-one, free sessions that focus on whatever the business is in need of. It could be help with a business plan, feedback on an idea, support with an existing business looking to expand, or help with their marketing. Whatever it is they need I can help, and if I can't, we have the network of contact that can.

42 FINDING YOUR NICHE

If you are interested in taking the same journey I suggest you find a few books to read on the topic of Becoming a Key Person of Influence. I mentioned one here several times, but I am sure there are others out there. There are a few examples of finding your niche out there, and all you have to do is Google it as I just did while writing this. Although I know mine here is one of many pages on what Google shared with me: Entrepreneur was the first to pop up and displayed "Find Your Niche in 60 Minutes or Less with these 4 Questions"

1) Identify the talents and skills you're good at.

2) Out of the above talents and skills, what do you enjoy doing most?

3) Of those talents and skills, what do people need?

4) From the above needs, what will people pay big money for?

It says that answering these questions shouldn't take you

longer than 60 minutes. But no matter how long it takes you, 60 minutes or a weekend, you need to figure it out if you want to become a key influencer. But as I've said, please keep one thing in mind if you're doing this just for the money: you may get bored with that. However, if you're doing it to help someone that makes all the difference.

For example, I do this because it will enable me to become known, and if I become known then people will want help. It could be that they need money, it could be that they need advice, it could be that I help a charity, but you should have a reason other than for the money.

If you do not think you have anything you can specialize in then think again. Here is some brief information on a young man named Caleb Maddix, the extraordinary entrepreneur who is currently 14 years old and is in all the major magazines. The latest I've seen with him is an interview on Forbes.com explaining how he has already accomplished becoming an entrepreneur and motivational speaker.

I also saw him on Grant Cardone TV this morning talking about how he knew this is what he would do at an age earlier than he already is. He said he told his father at age six he wanted to play baseball and his dad, who was a motivational speaker, told him, okay, if that's what you want to do then you can do it. The next morning his father woke him up early around 5am banging pots and pans to wake him up and asked are you sure this is still what you want to do and he said yes. From them on they got up every morning at 5 am for a year, and he became, the best ballplayer in the area because he practiced and practiced until he perfected his craft.

That's what this is all about: perfecting my craft. For me, I didn't have the resources to realize what it was. So I finally have a clear picture of what I need to do and I Connect Business, People, and Product through paid arranged meetings using my own proven system. So next I want to share how I go about arranging meeting using all of the older techniques from years back that still work today, but now adding in the latest with social media, explaining how that has changed it as well.

It is always evolving and we must stay on top of what technology has to offer as well. It's all the tools available that makes it easier, faster, and gives us all more visibility. This has served me well now for seven years, and I am always adapting. Sometimes people think I am crazy, and it's those folks that I somehow have to just do it anyway so that in the long run I will already have the proof by showing results. Sometimes those results take some time; some people are able to adapt quicker than others and are just a natural born salesman.

43 KNOWING THE PARTS OF THE SALE

There are a lot of parts to the sales process and many techniques to get things done in different ways, but for the most part there are steps and training for it all. Some people have trouble communicating, there is training for that; some have a tough time handling and overcoming objections and there is an actual technique to finding the real objection and sales training is going to teach you that as well. Imagine using the knowledge to bring out a real objection at home or in a relationship; how useful would that be, right.

I could talk about overcoming objections all day long but that's another area to focus on and right now is not the time, is that my real objection? Some people have problems closing the sale, asking for the sale, or knowing when they are receiving buying signs. It's amazing stuff, and although we say it's not a science, it's definitely a system, and it's defiantly something that requires training and assertiveness.

There is training on the approach, follow-up, taking notes, and managing it all. These are the areas I spend most of my time on and throughout the book you have heard me state, "That Nothing Happens Until The Meeting is Set and no business-to-business sale is ever made without an introduction." Isn't this kind of true in life? Think about it.

If you want to get to know someone you have to meet first. It's best that you do a little bit of research before setting it up. Then you meet over coffee and then there is the follow-up. It's the same thing in sales; it's a system whether you realize it or not. You're a sales person and everyone always has something to sell, so why not learn a little bit more about it. Or at least be able to recognize the flip side of this: if you're making a purchase you may be able to tell if the process is being used on you. A lot of purchasing agents go through sales training so they can identify what's going on inside the sales persons mind.

44 NETWORKING

One of my favorite ways to do prospecting for leads is through networking. We will talk about how this fits into the sales cycle when we get to the end. For now I want to share a few things on this topic, because maybe you are someone like me: someone who still wants to canvas, to get out of the office and away from the computer, and to be social. Yet at the same time, you're actually finding leads in a relaxed atmosphere where everyone one is on the same playing field. How cool is that?

I absolutely love networking and making new connections. I get to introduce people to other people who may be in need of a service or product, and that's the desire in me to help and it's easy. So what is networking anyway, and why am I focusing on it? It's a supportive system of sharing information and services among individuals and groups who have a common interest.

There is another benefit to learning networking, and I probably shouldn't say this, but it's a useful skill when you're at any type of event when you only have so much time to get to as many people as possible. If you're good at connecting people, you are able to get out of a conversation real easy just simply by bringing someone into the meeting that's just passing by, introducing the new person that I am talking with, and then moving on to the next prospect.

When networking, I am seeking to make as many connections as possible, exchange a business card, and start conversations. It's also good to have a "stand out from the crowd" pitch like I offered in earlier chapters. But at the end of the event, you should have collected quite a few business cards, and hopefully they came from someone that is a good prospect for your product or service.

Now you also have a possible lead to follow-up, and even if it's not a great lead, they may know someone who is. Lastly, its activity, and activity creates business. For some people all they ever do is networking, and I usually attend several a week. If you're in a larger city there is a possibility that you able to attend one every single night. The Chamber of Commerce in your city would be a great place to start, and the fees are pretty reasonable. If you're an independent contractor like me, you can get a really food deal because the fees are usually based on the size of the company.

Once you join, you can go to all kinds of training and they always have an introduction to the Chamber that is specific on how to take advantage of the membership. Remember their job is to get you the most exposure as you possibly can. They will usually assign you a Chamber Ambassador and this is the person that will join you on after hour's events, breakfasts, and annual meetings. There is a lot they can offer, and they can even become a liaison to introduce you and your services to another business or company.

All you have to do is ask. You can usually also acquire a Chamber list, and if you can get it electronically, you can load it into a database and start making planned visits. I have found these to be the easiest leads to produce. Not only that, you should add each person as a connection on LinkedIn so they can see all your updates. We will talk more about that when we get to the Social Selling.

When you are calling on a Chamber member account you will have taken the cold out of the call. I meant it's still technically a cold call until you have confirmed sometime of agreement, such as a meeting, or they have asked you for information. I recommend attending every event you can and even scheduling a Chamber event of your own.

You can sponsor an after-hours or before hours event. Even if you're a solo contractor, you can team up with another member with whom it makes sense and sponsor an event together. You will be able to address the entire crowd with a speech about you and your services. There is usually some money involved because you're the host, and most successful events will have food and drinks, so be prepared for that as well.

Another great activity you can attend, and that I recommend, is Speed Networking. This is an event that's usually an hour or two, where you and a large number of others will meet. You will have only a few minutes to give a quick pitch about who you are and what you offer and exchange a business card and literature. Then the timer goes off and you move onto the next person.

It's usually set up with tables and is a very quick way to get contacts. The ones I have attended are like three-minute sessions with around 20 people. Like all events and networking, you have to follow-up. So many people do not follow-up and wait for the phone to ring or an email to come across from someone you met, and if they are any good it probably will happen. Otherwise, why attend and waste your time? The object is to get leads.

But let's talk for a moment about the follow-up. If you receive a business card the next step is to give them a call or send them an email a day or two later to ask them to meet with you. Usually you should add a spin to it and say something to the effect that "I would like to get better acquainted with less distractions of the event," because it's usually chaotic and loud and is not the place to get to serious lead. Besides you do not have the time anyway. Plus, remember to take notes with each person you meet. They may also know someone even if they are not a great prospect for you.

Exchanging referrals is powerful because you now have a name doing the referring. But most important of all in this topic, or in any part of the sales process, is make sure you follow-up and do not wait for your phone to ring, or you are wasting your time and recourses.

45 SOCIAL MEDIA AND SOCIAL SELLING

Social Media and social selling is kind of new in the perspective of selling, at least for me as someone who has been at the game all his life. Social selling is a major player today, and if you have not adopted it you will have to start now. A lot of times today's buyers and prospects have already made a decision on who they may choose to buy from just by looking for you online, and if you're not there, then you miss out all together, or if your profile is not up-to-date and if it has a picture of you cooking out or in a T-Shirt prospects are probably going to move on. I am primarily talking about LinkedIn, which is not the same as Facebook, where you can get away with that type of stuff.

However, I have made it a point that since I am raising my profile I have the same professional picture on all of my social media sites so that it matches. If prospects happen to be doing a search for me across different platforms, it make it easy to identify myself. Plus, I have even started to clean up my Facebook profile as well. Not that there was anything bad at all. I am talking about watching what I post. Nowadays it's mostly inspirational and business-oriented things, but I do plan on creating and launching a new Facebook page when this book is published to help promote sales and generate leads.

Social selling is a two-way street because you can interact with clients on different platforms such as LinkedIn, Twitter, and Facebook. Video and real time streaming is even becoming more popular, and you had better know what it can do for you, because I can assure you your competition may already be on board.

Building an audience, friends, connections, and followers can also take some time, so it's best to get started now. But at the end of the day it's another way to prospect for leads. By posting relevant content on social media you become the expert and offer free information, and customers can get information easily, comment, ask questions, and become engaged.

You can even offer specials and contests so they stay tuned and keep checking back. LinkedIn has come a long way. Some may remember it being launched and using it as a way to search for a job, but it's evolved into so much more than that. It now allows me to keep track of my connections and their jobs, if they move around, and their company news and highlights so I can stay better informed. Plus it will notify you or birthdays and work anniversaries, and I can send a quick note and later they remember that.

But most of all, I can search connections and go right to the contact of the company and message them without ever leaving the office. And if you do not know them you can use another connection to have them introduce the two of you. LinkedIn also shows prospects your complete profile and expertise, endorsements from other clients, and recommendations. This goes back to them making a decision before you even make the call because they can look at what you have done and who you are all before 9:00am.

More on this being used in the sales process is coming up, but for now it's just a reference of what has changed. According to sources at LinkedIn, Sales professionals who use LinkedIn for social selling are 51% more likely to exceed their sales quota than sales professionals who don't use LinkedIn for social selling. But remember, social selling is not actually selling so don't be salesy. Your job is to create a relationship by offering advice and expertise not information about your company's products and solutions. Just be an expert in the field you're in.

Also, according to LinkedIn only 4% of B2B buyers said they would have a favorable impression of a salesperson who reached out cold. While 87% of the B2B buyers said they would have a favorable impression of a sales person who was introduced to them through someone in their professional network. So all in all, get your profile set up immediately, have a professional profile picture, update all the fields in your work history, and start making connections.

46 TRADITIONAL COLD CALLING

For those who have not adopted social selling and or live in a rural area where using online sites is just not something they do yet, you can still rely on traditional cold calling. Cold Calling is a loose term and does not always mean beating the streets and going door-to-door.

No one should be doing actual cold calling anymore, even if you are not on social media sites. It is just looked upon as unprofessional. I have been Cold Calling for the bulk of my career, but not the old Cold Calling where you do not know who you are looking for; now that's a real Cold Call and as mentioned not recommended.

What I am talking about doing is having information and research on your prospect before you even leave the office so that when I walk-in I sound like I know who I am after, because I usually do, and no one ever questions the walk-in when you ask for a certain person anymore. I would never walk-in without a contact name and that warms the call and now since social media started becoming available I can usually find a mutual connection.

I do still work in an area that is still adopting it as a means of approaching a client, so I still have to mix in the old ways. Besides, I actually like visiting clients. No matter how you do it, it's necessary and is the first step towards arranging a meeting.

I will talk more about cold calling in the next section of the book as we go through a step-by-step process, which will include how to integrate social networking and social selling. But the cold call to me is all about making a call without an appointment, and the appointment is what you are after. It sounds counter intuitive. Sometimes you will even receive an opportunity to meet right then and there. We will talk about how to handle that situation as well.

A cold call is an unsolicited visit or telephone call made by someone trying to sell goods or services. Some people also do cold calling on the telephone and email. Either way, it's cold if they have no idea you will be reaching out to them or don't know who to ask for. There are steps to take too get to a meeting and this is the first step of the process. You can't skip this and hope to get to a sale. Keep in mind, there is even training on telemarketing. I will show you how I use the phone and email to get to the meeting because they are both important steps in the process, depending on how it all goes.

Add to all of this you have to remember you're a professional, so being prepared shows you're serious and know what you are doing. Being prepared is only part of what you have to keep in mind, though, because you will need to know what to say and how to use body language. You even need to be dressed professionally to be taken professionally in a business sales call anyway. Yes, it all makes a difference. I will go into great detail about how to prepare for the cold call. I am basing the five steps on my career, on my training, and on my own knowledge and experience as to how customers have reacted and the fastest way I've found they will reply. I also have tried all the other ways people will show you and train you as the most effective way to acquire a meeting.

I still use these step-by-step action items today to connect people, business, and products together and it all starts with generating a lead.

This is 25 years of business development experience, an estimated 25,000 sales calls, and seven years of field testing my sales lead system for generating a meeting called *Effective & Proven Techniques for Acquiring New Sales Meetings!*

1) The Cold Call Preparation

-What you need to do to prepare for a cold call

2) The Cold Call Approach

-What to do when you walk-into a new prospects place of business unannounced or approach them using social selling

3) Asking for the Meeting

-How to go about setting up the meeting and various ways it may happen

4) Meeting the Prospect

-What you want to accomplish at the meeting

5) Database Management or CRM

-Keeping track of the prospects you meet and the meeting notes

Cold Call Preparation

Getting prepared for your cold call is fairly simple, but it will take some planning on your behalf if you want to have a career in sales and be effective at it. There are many ways to go about gathering information today. I always recommend having a contact name before you walk-in the door. Send an email or start making any phone calls first and it will make your life that much easier and will go a long way in meeting with the right prospect. Knowing who you are looking for is very important.

Remember, most, but not all gatekeepers (the person who answers the phone or the person at the front desk), are asked not to give out company information or names, etc. Remember, they receive tons of calls, walk-ins, and emails on a daily basis, so you can appreciate their reasons. If you're a decision maker, buyer, owner, or the manager, you don't have time to just drop what you're doing every time someone wants to make contact with you.

Most of the gatekeepers will ask you to leave your information behind and someone will contact you if they are interested. If I am cold calling and walking in, I actually agree with them and I will tell you why very soon. If you have been trained or are trying to walk-in and meet right then and there, I say good luck with that! I am a professional and respect everyone's time, and I want to set up a meeting. In a confirmed meeting you will have the proper attention and at a time that you both deserve as a seller and as a customer. Everyone's time is valuable so do not diminish yours either.

There are a lot of FREE sources today to get information about your prospects. Here is a list: your company database or file system, your local Chamber of Commerce if you're a member, tips club or other similar networking group's, social media like LinkedIn, Twitter, or Facebook, tradeshows, websites, or simply searching the internet. You can buy lists as well depending on your budget, but I gather most of the information I need to prospect online for free with LinkedIn, my client database, Manta.com, or by going directly to the company website you are researching.

We have recently started using LinkedIn Sales Navigator, which is a paid service, but I want everyone to know that this is not an endorsement for LinkedIn by any means. I have no ties to them other than the use of creating my profile just like the other 400 million business people using the site. It's just that over time it has evolved into offering a way to manage and gain leads, because just about everyone is on it now. I use Facebook and Twitter as well because they also have become great tools, and we will talk more on that very soon.

A lot of websites today will have all of the contact information you will ever need. Another very simple and old idea for suspects is to take notice of businesses as you pass by them, vehicles, advertising, or any news about a company. Have paper and a pen handy and write them down for later use and research. There are many other online resources out there today on the web, and some specialize in specific market niches.

All you have to do is Google for it. Hoovers.com, dnb.com, SalesGenie.com, and SaleForce.com are all great sources for sales leads. These sites usually charge a fee, as does LinkedIn Sales Navigator. I prefer the FREE information, but some are very budget friendly and are only dollars a day when you break it down.

The more you know about your prospects, the better your chances are at being successful with Cold Calling! When researching a company you should learn what type business they are in, the size and locations, who your contact is, or who can be an influence or a reference in helping you. Some customer websites not only list who the contact is especially government accounts and their email addresses.

If you're using a social site like LinkedIn, you can just do a search of the company and all the employees will come up. In the case for me with Prairie Tech, I am usually looking for the

I.T. Manager (Information Technology). Once you have found the contact name you can look to see if you have a mutual acquaintance and ask them to introduce the two of you, which really carries a lot of weight and creditability and will take the coldness right out of the equation as a reference.

References are as good as gold and it can all be done with LinkedIn InMail. Another way, which is not always recommended, is to send them a connection request. Without mutual acquaintances, however, they may be reluctant to accept your request. I would prefer the second party referral first, but if not and you do send a request, make some reference to someone you both know. I will talk about how to do that and the next steps later.

Now let's skip to a walk-in and assume the company does not have an online profile and you do not know the name of the person you are looking for. If it's a walk-in type of cold call you are setting up, then you will need a lot more information like the business's name, address, telephone number, and email address before making an attempt to reach out. You are now ready to spend the day Cold Calling. Make sure you have a list of at least 20. Put them in order and map it out into geographical areas. You do not want to drive 50 miles for one Cold Call and then go back to your office or home for another, etc. I use the GPS on my phone or computer and locate the nearest ones all together.

If you plan on doing this on a regular basis you will need a system, and you will eventually get used to it, and it will become second nature. You need to have plenty of business cards, and I recommend having a brochure about your company products and services. I even go a step further and include a pad and pen. I find these items will spark a conversation with the gatekeeper, and sometime they will even ask you for an extra.

You want the gatekeeper to warm up to you because they

are your liaison between you and the prospect you are trying to meet. They may even have something nice to say about you when passing it along. These tools will come in handy later on in the process. I do not recommend just randomly walking up and down streets without planning it first.

Do not waste your time or theirs, if you are not prepared or having a bad day. In the case of waking up to or having a bad day, just don't do it. There are days when I wouldn't want to buy anything even from myself, if I am having a bad day. I suggest those days for researching more suspect leads.

The whole point of this part is to make sure you know who you are looking for and want to meet with. Remember it can be a layer or two down from the actual person you are seeking, and that is okay because you are going to work your way up through the channel of command. As you do you will have the names and referrals of those who helped you, and it will add credibility. But as a professional, please DO NOT EVER walk-in, call, or email and say I do not know who I am looking for, unless you have exhausted all efforts to find out on your own first.

The Cold Call Approach

Once you have your prospecting list, what you now have is a list of suspects. They are technically not classified as prospects until you have received some type of agreement from them to meet with you or have asked to receive additional information or ask for more information or pricing on your product or service. However you are one step closer. With your prospecting list in hand you are almost ready to approach your fist Cold Call. But first you should have an idea of what you would like to say. Some people wing it and lord knows that I have. I have found that it is best to get your walk-in speech down before opening the first door. Let's start with what you could use for a Cold Call after you walked in unannounced and then we will sketch an email or social media version. Some call it the elevator pitch. Here is an example I use:

"Hello my name is _____ and I am with _____. I would like to ask if I can leave my business card and company information for Mr. or Mrs. Prospect. I do not have an appointment today; however, if you would be so kind as to make sure he or she receives it, I would appreciate it…. I will call again in a few days for an appointment."

Make sure you leave them with your business card and your company brochure. I also encourage specialty items like a pad or pen, because I personally receive higher meeting acceptance rates when I include all of these items. They are better informed when you do your next follow-up. There are still a lot of variables at this point, meaning you may already know them or they may already be a customer, and you are just wanting to increase your sales potential. You may have a new product or service you want to introduce or just have not seen them in quite some time and do not want to lose them to the competition. In any case, you have now planted a seed or spiked the prospect since you have visited them. I have a lot of things I call it. It is all part of the Cold Call.

Since you have the contact name, it is not as cold as you think. The gatekeeper rarely asks me anything with regards to what this is about, and they typically have no idea how well I really know the person I am looking for. The impression you want to give is that you are important and know what you are doing! Sometimes general conversation with the gatekeeper is good, but depends on how they respond.

Remember to always smile and dress professionally. If you are having a bad day, try again tomorrow or after lunch. There are entire seminars on motivation and in some rare occasions the person you meet when you walk-in is the contact person. So you should always be prepared to present your company and service on the spot if you must. I mentioned earlier in the chapter I would reference this part. The part where they could say I have time to meet now, and whenever possible I will try to ask for an alternate date and time so that we are not rushed or end up presenting your product or service in the lobby or waiting area.

An attorney wouldn't do this, so why should you? But, hey, if you get the impression it's now or never and your instinct kicks in, go for it. I just prefer an agreed on time and date that fits you both, and I would prefer an official appointment. You are showing courtesy and your professionalism.

Once you leave you should make notes on your cold call sheet on items such as the person who greeted you or maybe you were told they will be gone on vacation or you are informed that person is no longer there. I have even been advised that the person I am looking for is not the right contact, so before you leave ask the gatekeepers for a business card of the contact person. You will need the email address when following up.

When this happens it is okay. You didn't know they are gone and the information you have is the latest and, again, it showed that you knew who it was previously and this event creates a great conversation piece. Also, remember the gatekeeper's name because you will use it in your follow-up as another reference point. We will talk about the importance of this very shortly.

If you are approaching the suspect from social media there are two things that could have triggered a contact, especially if you're using social selling properly. I am talking about the fact that hopefully you're putting out content that is relevant, educational, and can get a response or create a conversation.

Or the vice versa. The more common role is that you are following their company and maybe they are creating content and you have responded to an article, and by doing so, you are showing yourself as an expert and that conversation may result in a follow-up to set a meeting. Another way to approach it is by reaching out and asking the person to connect with you directly so that you are a connection.

Obviously this is the best but how can you approach it versus just sending a request to connect? You can write something like this is the request.

"Hello my name is _____ and I am with _____. I hope you are having a great day and do not mind me reaching out. I noticed we both have 10 mutual acquaintances on LinkedIn, and although I could ask Mr. or Mrs. _____ to introduce us, I figured it was just as easy to reach out myself. Would you have 15-20 minutes sometime in the next week or two for a brief business introduction? I would use the time to introduce my company and myself. I would also like to get better acquainted with you and your operations so the opportunity is mutual. Would Monday at 9am or Tuesday at 2pm work best for you. Please let me know. I will look forward to your reply. Kind Regards, your signature and company information inserted here.

That is a pretty straightforward request and non-threatening approach and seems pretty harmless. If I know they are a chamber member or part of a group we both belong to, I might even mention it, especially if it's a Chamber of Commerce group because that is for networking. Why become a member be if you're not going to network? Be careful how you say it, though, because you do not want to come across as pushy or make them feel stupid.

Asking For the Meeting

This portion of acquiring a new sales lead is for the time when you walked in the day prior and left information and gathered information yourself. Remember the introduction earlier? This is now handled the next day when all the door-to-door activity is done and you are back at the office. You may spend two or even three days in the field Cold Calling or on sales meetings. The more, the better you will increase your odds of securing a sale. Later on as you get ramped up and you are setting up meetings, you will need more time to mix in new sales calls and social selling to keep your funnel full.

I feel this is the stage that will make or break the chances of you getting the meeting and making a lead out of it. I always like to do my first follow-up via email and combine phone calls as a secondary option, and now you can even mix in social media. It all depends if I have their email address or not. In my follow-up email, I am asking for an appointment, and I am informing the prospect that I stopped by a few days earlier and that I left my business card and company information with their staff.

I tell them that I hope they received it, that I hope they do not mind my follow-up, and that I would like 10-15 minutes of their time for a brief business introduction, just like I did with the InMail on LinkedIn earlier. I always give them several days to pick from, as well as several times, because if you just put one out there, you have decreased your chances, and then you have more back and forth messages. I recap a little bit about who I am and whom I work for. If we are fellow chamber members in that area I mention it as well or maybe we have done business in the past.

Later on when you are on your second cold call with them, your message will be a little different and you will let them know you have tried before, and list the month and year. And this is true if it was done using social media. Make sure you keep a record of it all and we will discuss this in step five. This will add a lot of weight to the message and will really let them know you are keeping track and have a lot of interest in meeting with them.

If the gatekeeper gave you anything to mention such as a

referral or a name you will want to mention this as well. Be very specific. End the email message telling them you will look forward to their reply. Add a best regards or kind regards in your message and all of you contact information such as address phone number and email and now your social media links. Here is an example:

Good afternoon Mr. or Mrs. Prospect,

I know you are by appointment only, so I stopped by yesterday and left my business card and company information with your staff. I hope you received it and do not mind my follow-up. I would like to ask for 10-15 minutes next Thursday or Friday at 10:00am or any time after that. I would like to give a brief introduction about our group, get acquainted, and learn more about your business as well, so the opportunity is mutual. It seems these days when networking in the local business community, there is always reciprocal opportunities. Lunch is even an option.

We are (describe who/what you are) and we like to network with organizations like yours. Our company is a well-established family organization promoting business locally, and we are fellow chamber members as well. Thank you for your time and consideration, and I will look forward to your reply and direction.

Kind Regards,

Full Name

Company Name

Contact Information

Social Media Information

See how easy that flowed and made sense. You recapped on everything. Remember, if the gatekeeper gave you his or her name, mention it. Use that leverage in your second reply such as: *I left my business card and company information with* _____ *and he/she said they would make sure you received it.*

In any case, remember you will receive some replies but most will not reply at all. They will either feel you are selling something not mentioned that they do not need, already have a relationship with a similar company, are too busy, not interested, or just forget. I wait a day or two, and then do my follow-up number two via the telephone or social media. If I am able to get through to them, I recap on just about everything that was in the email and ask for the meeting. Then the third and fourth follow-up attempt is staggered out over a few more days. Each time and I repeat the email with the first email attached and shorten the message with; sorry I missed you, and I did stop by, and I did send an email or called, and I give specific dates and who I talked with at the time.

Again, I am being very specific, and by now they know I am not a spammer and that I will probably keep trying. Keep in mind, if you have access to LinkedIn Sales Navigator or a similar online business social media account, you can always include that as one of your attempts, but always let them know you have already tried, when you tried, and how you tried. Be a good record keeper. Remember this is your business and your livelihood.

At this point, if they are really not interested after about four staggered follow-up attempts, you either will get a reply or you will have to understand you are not their priority at this time. Try not to take it personal, because there can be a million reasons for not receiving a reply.

You want to be persistent and assertive but you do not want to be a pest. Just keep in mind, there is always another day, and you will try again. This is all part of this entire process, and you will not be giving up. Six months to a year later, you will repeat the entire process all over again and will have an even more dramatic message, because you will have tried in the past and will be able to list specific dates and are still very interested.

In the follow-up attempt six months to a year later, you may also be asking them to kindly point you to the right contact or ask for assistance with the direction. The more this goes on into the second or third year, eventually they will most likely meet with you, and it is typically because of your persistence. This is not to say it will take years; most of the time it will happen sooner.

This is your career so do not be looking at this as a short-term opportunity. It's for a lifetime, no matter what type of sales you are in. I have been contracting for Prairie Tech now for seven years, so you can imagine the repetitive information I have built up after stacking 52 weeks a year on top of the next year and the year after that.

Eventually you will be so busy doing follow-up and setting up reoccurring meetings, you may feel like you have very little time to keep adding new business opportunities. This may be where social media and social selling may come into play, as well as account management. But never forget you will always need new business and you will always need new accounts and prospects, so you have to do time management and split your week up into allowable times for every step.

After the first week of this activity you should see three to four set meetings. My goal is to set the meeting, and I am not selling a product or service at that time. I am selling the appointment! If I try and sell a product or service I will most likely get a "no" reply more frequently, and the odds will dramatically decrease. There are those occasions where timing is perfect and the moon is aligned just right, and I have walked in on a cold call unannounced and the very next and first actual meeting end up assessing the needs only to find out they have been seeking quotes on the exact service we offer and we make the sale. Anything is possible and this is why you have to also make sure you have everything you need with you.

You do not want to excuse yourself and seem unprepared and ask if you can run to the car to get what you need. It doesn't look good; it looks unprofessional. Why make it harder on yourself. I would much rather get the meeting than not meet them at all. You have to start someplace, and if you want to sell your product or service you will need to get the meeting.

I use SMEs (Subject Matter Experts) on my next step meeting, which for me requires an extra step. I know in technology or very complicated sales you may as well need to as well, so let me touch on that very quickly. In my case we offer an assessment. This is a great door opener and is something you can add to your general introduction.

Remember, each time you meet you want to sell the next meeting and always ask for permission. So once I am at the general introduction, I usually walk through our services very briefly so that I leave enough time to ask questions of interest and ask questions about their current business and current suppliers, and then I talk about the assessment and offer a next meeting. This is when I bring in my SME. I am also the one who arranges the next meeting and you have to coordinate that with the customer and the SME, so sometimes it gets a bit tricky. But after a while you get really good at it, and the SME becomes more flexible because they know you are working for them and generating business. Activity is the key to this whole process.

The more people you reach out to, the more follow-up you will have, and the more leads you will produce. Even the one that you run into that doesn't want anything or may need service, you should still assist and set it all up. Activity is king;

and do not forget referrals. Everyone knows someone one else, so do not be afraid to ask.

Later in the fifth section of this, I will talk about keeping track of all the notes and follow-up needed for this so you will be organized. If you are repeating this process you will set up meetings and you will get busy.

Meeting the Prospect

So by now you have some meetings arranged, and let's assume you're at the meeting. What do you want to accomplish? Many sales experts will say you want to make the sale or get the business, and you do. I think it is fair to say this is what everyone wants when making sales calls. I have learned over the years there are different types of sales people, different markets, and different prospects, so you have to find what best fits you, your style, and your marketplace. What works in Peoria, IL may not work in New York and vice versa.

In my opinion, you have to always ask for permission in the sales process: permission to move to the next step. If you have approached the prospect professionally, followed up in a timely fashion, and had a convincing message as to why they should meet with you, then you have done your job acquiring a new sales lead.

When you go to the meeting remember what you told them in the beginning when you sent the first follow-up email or made that first telephone connection. In my case, about half of my meetings are arranged as an introduction for me, the company, and our products and services. I know this approach will get me much further than trying to make an appointment to sell something, because unless you're hard selling or happened to be calling on them at the right time, you will find it much easier to get the meeting by offering a brief introduction. I learned this the hard way and after trying hundreds of times with the other ways you're taught. I do want to sell something, but I cannot skip the steps.

As you introduce yourself, offer a handshake and thank them for having you in to meet, then you can start in with a brief business introduction or even some quick small talk. Small talk could be a recap of something that was said by the gatekeeper you met or something you saw in the office or something you read on a social media post—anything that you feel is relevant without wasting a bunch of time. We will cover the time aspect here in a few moments. Remember you only asked for 15-20 minutes, so you need to stick to it. If they want to give you more time they will give you the signal by talking long after you are done, and you can always sense if they have a busy day.

Most will tell you so, and with others, you just need to respect their position. In a meeting like this, I want to ask for a status update on where they stand today with the products or services I provide from my competition. This is non-threatening, and it works well into the conversation as long as you ask permission. In some cases the prospect will just tell you everything you are looking for, or they may tell you they are interested in a specific product or service you offer. If they do, Bingo, you hit the jackpot! Remember the ones who let you walk through your presentation and do not offer any information about themselves are possibly complying with your request for a simple introduction, or they truly have no interest in buying anything anytime soon. Do not worry.

You have still made a new contact and will see them again when you repeat the process later on. In my experience there is always something to discuss about what you offer, and it may be one to three years later. But if you will be making a career out of selling, you will appreciate the lead even then. The cycle of this is such that the odds are you will have plenty of other sales possibilities in your sales funnel anyway.

I have had more opportunities than I can mention where there was absolutely no interest at the time of the meeting but yet the very next day I've had email and phone calls asking me to arrange a meeting because something has come up or something crashed the night prior, so do not count anything out and leave the meeting with an open-door feeling and generosity.

If they are interested in your product or service, ask to set up another meeting by giving them alternative dates and times again, then return prepared to offer a full assessment of whatever it is you are selling, and bring the proper SME with you.

Depending on your type of business you may need to bring experts back in with you for the second meeting, and it could be a manager or owner, but make sure you are clear by repeating what was established. This will get the client in full agreement that we are returning for another meeting to accomplish X. In my line of work with the businesses I represent, this is how we do it. After the assessment or initial discussion of their wants and needs, you can now offer a proposal or scope of work to be performed.

Your ability to close a sale is a whole separate seminar. Whether they buy on the spot or not will determine your next follow-up attempt. In any case, congratulations, you have been on a solid meeting and a solid sales call. Do not forget to take a lot of notes and gather details. As I said, if you are in a technical business and the subject matter is the one doing all the work I still go on the call because I want to know as much as I can and the learning never stops.

When you go on call after call, you get better and better, and that's what the topic of my book is really about. It's about learning what you've learned and having eventually done it so much that you become an expert at it. Then you can claim your fame. So what about all these notes, meetings, all the contacts, and the extra specialists you need; when to call back, what was said, what did the gatekeeper say, and what did the decision maker say; what objections do they have, what is the next meeting about and the list goes on. How do you manage all of that information? Well you can't personally do it you will need a CRM Customer Relationship Management System or Database.

Database or CRM Management

Database Management or having a CRM is critical in the whole process of cold calling and selling; you cannot wing it by just writing things down the old way on paper and stack it all up on your desk or a box. I can say this with evidence because way back in the day, that's how I did things. Even managing a large household sometime requires a system, even if it's a calendar to put dates and notes on. Throughout the discussions I have mentioned taking notes, doing a follow-up, or capturing names, emails, and follow-up times and meetings you have arranged, etc. So you need a place to store all this information and a system that will remind you of everything.

There is no way you can effectively keep track otherwise. At my current position as a business development contractor, we have used several forms from a web-based program called Highrise to a software-based program called ACT. There are quite a few out there, and all you have to do is search for them online or contact me directly for more information. I see Sales Force.com all the time, but haven't used it yet. Plus we have a new custom-developed program with one of the Prairie Technology alliance members called Facet Trak, and it does everything and more along with being a ticketing system.

The database, or some call it CRM (Customer Relationship Management), will be your best friend in sales. It will allow you to merge other data information you may already have.

You can add new contacts and notes from your meetings and cold calls.

We talked about follow-up a day or two, and again in six to twelve months, and even three years later. When you do this you want to look back on your notes and be able to tell the prospect or client what you remember about the last attempt or the last meeting. Many of the cold call follow-up attempts will be deferred by the prospect, and they will ask you to call again another time. These are golden opportunities, and I like using email messages I receive from them when they tell me this. I use that same older email when I do my follow-up so that it reminds them of what they asked me to do, as opposed to me just contacting them again, and they may have forgot.

Some ask you to follow-up again later because it is easy to get you to stop bothering them. Others may hope that you forget about the follow-up and you may never call again. I like showing them that they asked me to follow-up, which is why I like email so much.

Other parts of the database will allow you to store your quotes or proposals. It should also allow you to track and analyze your prospects and customers by geographical areas, or by categories and zips codes that you can later use when canvassing again. Remember the database is going to allow you to be effective and continue the cycle of acquiring new leads.

Odds are that three to four people out of 20 visited will see you, but the other 16-17 you will try again and again over the years until you have received a "no thanks," are told to stop, or you get the meeting. The database will also allow you to market to them via direct mailers or e-newsletters. These are additional marketing efforts that will net you additional business. For more information here, you may contact me directly, as well for advice and recommendations. If you stay with this and repeat the process, you can't lose. It does work. You will even get to the point where you feel you have too much on your plate, and when that happens, you can adjust the input and adjust the amount you put into the front end.

THE AUTHOR

My name is John McKee, age 53. I've spent the last 26 years of my life in business development and sales. Twelve years of this time was dedicated to starting four new businesses of my own, working as a contractor with several other startups, and working for four Fortune 500 companies. I have credited myself with over 25,000 sales calls and meetings and tens of thousands of hours in which I was ultimately responsible for connecting people, business, and product through arranged meetings. I've asked thousands of people for meetings to present a business, product, solution, or service, and it's all been at either the front door of the homeowner's house, their business office, through an email, on the telephone, or at a social networking event. Sales professionals like me have been taught over the years that we are all hired to sell products and services; and that is true of most and is all part of what I've been doing for as long as I can remember. However, what is unique about me is that I view the beginning of the sales process a little differently than most others. I see this as the most valuable part of opening new doors and creating new opportunities. I will discuss this in more detail throughout this book. I will share my ideas and what I have learned from a lifetime of sales calls. I'm currently being paid to arrange business meetings for six technology companies in Central Illinois, and I absolutely enjoy it. I have the opportunity to meet new people and help others. I have my own mantra: I believe nothing ever happens until the meeting is set, and no sale is ever made without an initial confirmed information meeting. This puts me in a very secure position because every business needs to meet new customers and every business needs to grow. There are many books and articles written about the importance of sales, and you will always find the most important business skill every entrepreneur must have is Sales Skills! I ask you: how do we make a sale in business? We arrange a meeting for the introduction. I'm writing this book because I want to share with all of you what it's like to spend a lifetime in business sales searching for new opportunities in business, what this has done for me, how it has created new opportunities outside of sales, and I feel it translates into a good book. I will talk about the changes taking place in cold calling like social selling. I share my point of view that life is not a straight line; it's more like unexpected twists and turns. I will discuss how I ended up developing my own product to sell and how that led me to writing a book. In doing so I figured out what my specialty is. In the end I explain what I plan to do in my field of expertise by creating my own niche as a Key Person of Influence. You will hopefully get to know me through my personal life stories. It has been quite a journey, and although it's just life happening, I write because I can, and I want to take the time before it's too late. Before deciding to write this book, I honestly wasn't sure if I should stay in business development. Now that I have invented a product, maybe that's is where I should spend the rest of my life, helping create new products, helping others, or both. Wouldn't you like to know what your calling is? Maybe you already know, and if you are like me, and you are still wondering. There is a way to figure it out. The late and great Steve Jobs once said: "Creativity is just connecting things. When you ask creative people how they did something, they feel a little guilty because they didn't really do it, they just saw something. It seemed obvious to them after a while. That's because they were able to connect experiences they've had and synthesize new things."

JOHN MCKEE

Made in the USA
San Bernardino, CA
18 August 2016